the girl who cried FORGIVENESS

Vivia Leigh

the girl who cried
FORGIVENESS

Vivia Leigh

Have the courage to heal, and then
celebrate what you have overcome.

© 2020 by Vivia Leigh

All names of induviduals and businesses have been changed to protect the identities of characters in the story.

Edited by Debbie McMurray & Esther Kay
Book and Cover Design by Danika Noel
Photography by Molly Jane & Matt Grothe
Cover Art by Nicolette Vaughn

Vivia Leigh Books
Kansas City, Kansas
vivialeigh.com
Printed in the United States of America by BookBaby

Print ISBN: 978-1-09832-819-1

First Paperback Edition

Disclaimer:

You may be here during a time of hardship, if so, I encourage you to read slowly, and to be certain to utilize the worksheets as you read. If you do not use the book accordingly, then the stories might overwhelm you.

This book does not take place of therapy. While the stories and worksheets are theraputic, people need people, not a book on it's own. Please utilize "Finding Your Therapist" on page 94 to build onto your support system.

Vivia Leigh

contents of resources and worksheets

contents of resources and worksheets

contents of resources and worksheets

contents of resources and worksheets

other resources
& worksheets

f o r w a r d

DEBI JEAN MCMURRAY

I am inviting you to go on an extraordinary journey, perhaps one you've never been on before, and one you'll never want to go on again, yet you will, once you discover the freedom found. This journey is one that many will never experience as the young girl in this book who learns the power of forgiveness, yet no matter what your experiences in life, we all need this process in order to be free. Throughout the process, you will feel extreme emotions, as that of a person on a rollercoaster, riveting to extreme highs, then plunging to the bottomless lows. This is not a journey one would find delightful, yet the privilege to learn from one so young is an absolute blessing.

I met Vivia when she was 18-years-old. Our connection was not by blood, but by a bond that is greater than blood, and stronger than bone, for it is a divine connection, a spirit kinship, one that only God entrusts to us. This is the bond that I have with my beautiful friend, Vivia. I've often told her I'm her Momma Bear. I'm older, yet when we are together, we are simply "friends". I feel very protective of her, yet she's also protective of me, "for a friend loveth at all times."

We see each other's faults, flaws, strengths, weaknesses, and triggers, yet in spite of all, our love does not change. We rejoice over each other's victories, we cry over each other's sorrows. Vivia is a ray of dancing sunlight shining through the darkest clouds. On the worst possible day ever, she brings joy, happiness, laughter, and hope to anyone needing the light she brings. One cannot help but notice the beautiful aura around Vivia, for it simply captivates you. You can see it in her freedom, for she has found truth, acceptance, love, happiness, and of course joy. She radiates everything that is the exact opposite of what she has walked through in her life. She is an example of God's amazing love, and his wonderful restoration process.

I've often heard it said that those God uses the most have walked through the scorching fire, surviving the dark night of the soul. They, in turn, come forth as refined gold. During this refinement process, God is remaking them for his purposes, to be able to touch the lives of countless others. These are ones who have experienced much brokenness. They understand humility, and find their identity and self-worth not in their past experiences or tragedies, but rather in how those things affected their life and it's outcome. They realize it is the outcome of the strength lying within them, that causes them to rise up, stand firm, knowing their place in this life. They run toward their destiny, knowing nothing will ever stop them, and if knocked down, they will rise up, catch their breath, and keep running.

When I first met Vivia, I had no clue, at all of any of her story. She looks like the perfect person who has the perfect life. God divinely placed us in each other's lives. While I only saw the radiant, joyful persona of Vivia, I little by little began to learn of her past. My heart would break with her as more things happened and I walked with her through more pain. I must say, it was hard at times for me to watch the heartache she went through. There was a sadness as I watched my friend be accused of things that were totally false. However, I watched her become more determined than ever to overcome, succeed, and keep her dreams alive. I am so happy to look back over the

11

11 years I've known her and confidently say she has successfully done everything she started out to do. She never once deterred from the vision that God gave her. When the journey got tough, she never gave up, but kept going and never looked back. She pursued her path. She is victorious.

Another person would have probably thrown in the towel, but this is how the strong and the weak are separated. An interesting thing to note about Vivia is this: you will never see her feel sorry for herself, and she never once blamed God for anything that happened to her. That to me, in and of itself, is one of the most beautiful parts of her story. As you read her story, you will start to feel many emotions. If you're religious, you might be tempted to judge, if you hear her use an off-color word in this book, (one you might not like or approve of in your religious community,) I'd like to simply say for the record, from a pastor's daughter, "let us be kind, for we have never walked in her shoes."

You might even say you hate religion, and that's why you're judging, but let's also be careful careful here, for many who say that, are still very religious in hating religion, and they don't even recognize that attribute in themselves, that their hating religion has made them religious it's a bit of a catch 22, because to be religious can be very addictive. Let's just be frank about it, this really is true. Everyone's hallelujahs, "Praise the Lord's", and Amens, repetitively? We all know that everyone does this without even knowing why sometimes. I hope this book brings revelation to some of that, and brings much freedom, for if we remain there, we can help noone, including ourselves. You see, there are so many hurting, so many wounded, and one of those wounded could be you. I know Vivia would agree with me on this. If you are one of the wounded ones, if a person offended you by using the name of our Lord and says they are a Christian while offending you using his name, please do not hate Jesus because of their self righteousness. I will personally apologize for the Christian communities' actions myself. Many people say things without knowing why they said it. I know Vivia's heart is to bring her book to everyone, and her heart is as golden as anyone I know. This book is going to take you on a journey of many types of abuses, from sexual to spiritual to mind control, and everyone who has worked on this book with Vivia desires freedom for everyone reading the book. Here's the wonderful thing that happened to my beautiful friend, she learned to forgive.

If you look at the bible and the teachings of Jesus, psychology, quotes throughout history made by many people of many religions, and their teachers, there is one common thread that runs through all; Forgiveness is for you more than the one you forgave. So today, as you start this journey, I promise you, you need to be ready for the unexpected. Open your mind, heart, soul, and spirit, and be ready to see what forgiveness can do for you. Forgiveness enriches your life, makes you a better person, so you will be more fulfilled. Throw away any preconceived ideas, and just like "The Girl Who Cried Forgiveness", open your heart to this continual process.

DEBI MCMURRAY
l e t t e r   f r o m   t h e   e d i t o r

"A friend loveth at all times" Prov 17:17

If I were asked to describe my friend Vivia, I would quote this verse, for it fully describes her. Vivia loves, and with everything she has. She one-hundred percent, and whole-heartedly, gives all that she has, and never asks anything in return. There are very few people who have this gift in life and if you find a person like her, let me say, God has blessed you, for you have a faithful, forever friend.

I've known Vivia since she was eighteen, and when I learned more of her story, her past, and the things she walked through, it really made me stop, do a double take on her persona, and how one so young, surviving so much, could seem so whole, and put together. It is a total miracle. How could one go through so much, yet retain her joy, life-giving peace, happiness, love, spirit of forgiveness, compassion and passion for all. Vivia, in some miraculous fashion, found it within her to keep a pure heart, and live selfless and for others. That truly blew me away!

In today's world of selfish people, Vivia is one of the least selfish people I've met. She loves people, always looking for ways to help others, and I can truly say, she is making this world a better place. Vivia is an example of God's amazing love as she walks in grace and humility.

It has been my great honor to work with Vivia in editing this book. I am just one of many who has helped her bring her dream to life. As they say, it takes a village. I realize that with every project, you put your whole heart and being into it, and it literally becomes something that you birth. It is a hard thing to do when people come and give you their thoughts to change things because it's your baby that you have carried for so long.

Vivia has been so gracious and easy to work with, if we've said "how about this" or "how about that?", she has had an open mind. I have to give her great applause for that, because it's a very hard thing to do. She has been a great person to work with, and I just can't say that enough. I have worked with many hard-headed, stubborn, and unteachable people. Vivia has much to give, much to tell, and so many hurting people in this world, need to hear what she has to say.

In many ways, I feel like a second mother to Vivia. My heart is full for her and I love her. I am so happy to be a part of this book. It has been exciting to watch it come together! I would say to anyone out there, please read this book! I promise, you will be blessed. It will impact you in areas you never expected, because all of us have gone through times where it has been hard to forgive; While forgiveness is challenging, it is extremely powerful. Throughout my process as Editor, I was reminded of something a long time ago that I needed to let go of. I was able to forgive with Vivia's support, and able to move forward. Sometimes, it is good for us to reflect on our past and focus on things we are still holding onto, so that we may let go, forgive and move forward. Take your time going through this book, apply it to your life and find the freedom Vivia has even led me to!

Blessings,

ESTHER VIVIAN KAY
letter from the editor

In the summer of 2019, a few months after I first published the interview magazine Lacuna: The Missing Stories, Vivia reached out to me on Instagram congratulating me on the magazine, and wanting to be a part of it. Immediately, I knew I wanted to work with her, and felt sad to turn her down since I couldn't yet afford to pay writers. As I learned more about her and her vision, I wanted to be a part of what she is doing. One mission of Lacuna is to support people who are making a big difference in our societies.   When she told me about her book, I didn't hesitate to offer my help and expertise as an editor. We bridged oceans and time when working together on editing her book - Vivia, in the early hours of her day in the USA, and me, late in the evening in Germany.

When Vivia told me she was writing her autobiography, my first thought was that she is quite too young to tell the story of her life. The more we worked on editing her book, the more I understood that I was wrong. A life story is not written in years, but experience. Vivia has not only much to tell, she also has even more to give.

Vivia is an inspiration for the people who know her, will be an inspiration for every reader who picks up her remarkable book.

In "The Girl Who Cried Forgiveness", Vivia Leigh takes you by the hand, and on a journey into her past. With brave clarity she talks about her dysfunctional past and the abuse she had to endure. With her commitment to transparency, Vivia Leigh inspires us to leave behind the role of the victim, in order to become the heroine of our story. Rather than painting situations and people in black and white, "The Girl Who Cried Forgiveness" invites us to see the grey and colorful areas, where we are invited to transform ourselves. With Vivia's the courage to be vulnerable with the reader, he courage to become more vulnerable becomes more real than the pain that was so deep, and the walls slowly come down.

Vivia Leigh is the living proof that it is not only possible to forgive whoever harmed us, but also, by keeping forgiveness hilt into our foundation, it is our key to sustaining successful, healthy, sustainable relationships. Her own story is a testimony of healing. She also invites us to write our own stories. As you read this book and practice forgiveness, she invites you to write your own story. As you start to write, you will never feel alone.

"The Girl Who Cried Forgiveness" is not only a testimony of what is possible when we long to forgive, but it is also a practical guide with worksheets and inspirations that will help each person face their most painful moments triumphantly.

SARA PENDER
Licensed School Counselor

"I see how forgiveness has done so much for Vivia. I am constantly amazed by her spirit. She has more grit than many people I know, and I am so proud of her. From being a middle school student to the young woman she has become, I have watched her grow into herself over the years. I know she had struggles, and she talks about them openly in this book. Through everything she has been through, her faith has kept her grounded to what is important to her."

ZACK HENSLEY
Pastor

"Vivia remembered how many people wanted to sensationalize her story. This was the first time she'd really been invited and encouraged to take a step back. I encouraged her to take time to heal fully, so that she could share her complete story of redemption later on. It is incredible to see her move in this now, and in a way that sharing such personal depth heals her, and invites others to do the same without harm."

PHIL BOHLANDER
Liscensed Psychologist

"I met Vivia as a client. Vivia has written many blogs in relation to our sessions pursuing EMDR Therapy. While a Psychology Major at Avila University, and referred by a mutual friend, Vivia came to receive EMDR being both educated and prepared; without filter. Working with her has not been too difficult. Her transparency helps her healing journey extremely well."

CARI MADISON
Liscensed Psychologist

"I experienced a situation with Vivia where she struggled to put herself first, in a very trying relationship. Vivia has been transparent with me from the beginning of our friendship. We've truly helped each other in multiple hard times. When Vivia needed a therapist, or to understand more about her own anxiety and depression, we would talk together, and I would refer her to my best friends in my professional support system. Her strength and boldness, how she acknowledges her self worth, inspires me as much as she says I motivate and inspire her. It's a give-and-gain kind of friendship with Miss Vivia."

TERESA MCCLAIN
Psychology Professor

"I am a Psychology Instructor and a Sexual Assault nurse examiner, offering much support throughout the psychology industry. I met Vivia on campus and the first thing that stood out to me about her was that she is a very noticeably happy and optimistic kind of person; unstoppable. Whatever obstacles would come up, she would vent and then dive right into a solution for the situation; she makes lemons into lemonade and she's very good at it!

Vivia has an entrepreneurial spirit, and is able to build one idea onto another and engage people to shine with her and not beneath her. This is a rare trait, especially by someone who has endured as much as she has."

MIKE RIZZO
Liscensed Psychotherapist

"Vivia calls it a "curiosity train." What a great description! A few years ago, when we first met, I could see the pure heart, seeking truth, even though the odds were stacked against her. Her search was, and still is, clothed in mercy, as she seeks to meet everyone at their own unique place in the journey. I have seen the transformation in her heart and life, and a growing wisdom to rest a bit on the glory plateaus until they become a launch pad unto the next level."

MARY POPE
Oh Baby! KC, CEO

"It was a beautiful day in May 2019, Vivia and I had been Instagram friends for a short time, and had not yet met in person. We were both set up as vendors at a local mom-centered event with one booth between us. We met briefly in the midst of the busy-ness of speaking to moms and other business owners. During that brief, yet meaningful conversation, Vivia and I had a deep connection that happens between people with similar visions and purposes.

Our words resonated with each other and we became fast friends. Our goals of supporting moms who are struggling, need community and to feel like their best selves again, mirrored each other although our businesses were different, and we have since discovered that in supporting each other as colleagues and friends, we can better serve the women who lean on us for support. I am honored to have this opportunity to contribute to Vivia's writing and to offer a small portion of what I do to help families thrive."

DEAR READER,

WHAT SHOULD YOU EXPECT FROM THIS BOOK?

This is my truth and it is nobody else's truth but mine.

I own this experience fully. I seek to offer transparency, honesty, and perspective. In my personal story, I discuss different forms of pain and suffering, as well as different forms of healing which include coping mechanisms and resources. Readers may experience the same thing and take away very opposite stories, ideas, highlights, memories or even triggers. It is not anyone's job to fill the blanks of another's lived truth; all views are unique and should be respected. We should never live in a mindset to default to, "Why can't you just be like me?"

Dear Reader

WHAT IS THE PREMISE OF THIS BOOK?

This book exists to serve as an example of transparency for those in pain, so that they will feel understood, and perhaps not out-of-line or alone. The purpose of this book is to offer a new perspective from someone who's been a victim and who chooses not to remain a victim for her entire life. For people playing God, who might be critical of people in pain, please do not judge those who are trying to overcome victimization. Believe me, we judge ourselves already harshly enough. Please support these people as they process their experience, learn to take care of themselves, and work through the choices they have made to not seek revenge or live in anger.

WHAT IS THIS BOOK'S GOAL?

This book is about my forgiveness of others. This book does not exist to point fingers at anyone, to hold blame toward anyone, or to place myself on a pedestal. The name of every person, town, organization, street, and lake has been renamed as to protect those whom I have forgiven. I seek to build a gap between bitterness and pride, defensiveness and freedom, humility and forgiveness.

WELCOME TO MY JOURNEY.

Ultimately, I felt a calling to write this book. This book will hopefully continue my healing experience and bring closure to my inner demons. I write this book to offer to others a place of safety, a place of feeling and a place of boundary on their own healing journey. May my own story serve you as you begin yours; love and peace be with you!

When you love
When you care for others kindly, gently
and with grace,
Then something disrupts that peace,
That something brings a tidal wave of control and
manipulation harming you.
Your desire may be to erupt without
warning and with a superhero complex.

I've been there. I've wanted to declare certain people
unforgivable, toxic and ill-equipped to change for the
better.

Surrender. Pray. Forgive.
These people are not worth your time or energy.
We give more attention to those who hurt us than to
those who love us deeply.
The bitter and scared response stops here.
As I cry forgiveness, many will turn away and say,
"I don't need to forgive; this situation and this person
is different; unforgivable."
Is your righteous anger worth giving up the time you
could have to heal?
Is your pride worth losing yourself because you
cannot let go of a person who offended you?
Sometimes, it just takes God to change and impact the
hard things and soften your heart.
It takes you to forgive and regain true freedom from
the situation and a victim mentality.

INTERLUDE

I was born May 29, 1992, at 9:52PM, and was transferred from St. Mary's Hospital to St. Luke's Hospital 45 minutes away. I was meant to be a 4th of July baby, but I was ready to change the world earlier. I was born 4 pounds, 13 ounces, and 17.5 inches long. I was nicknamed Birdie. This nickname was inspired by my big robin egg blue eyes, and my ability to regurgitate after my tube feedings. In addition to not eating on my own, I could not breathe on my own, and was on a ventilator for two weeks. I was diagnosed with Hyper Thyroid Disease, and was lethargic. I was born and placed into a plastic cage, where much protection was demanded in order to see me. When my immediate family wanted to visit, they had to wash their hands for 7 minutes before diving into a gown to see me in the incubator. When my mother touched me, she had to use a forceful touch, so that I would feel it through the haze of lethargy. When I am told these memories, I feel like being incubated, and nurturing, may have been withheld from me. I stayed in the hospital for 8 weeks, until I weighed at least 6 pounds, and was able to go home to Mom, Dad and Sissy. After leaving the hospital, the lack of nurturing by my parents continued. Mom didn't hug or kiss me. Dad's touch was either inappropriate or repulsive. Neither of my parents gave me the positive physical touch I craved. Now, I am a bird set free. Never again will I be caged by the lack of nurturing or confined by the inability to be well loved.

Throughout my childhood, I created wonderful memories that I still cherish. In a "heard it through the grapevine" town, where everyone knows everyone's business, I made some sweet, kind, good friends. I could safely ride my bike all around town, from dawn to dusk, without concern. Neighbors genuinely cared about each other, and would keep a protective eye out for each other's families. Ironically, the only unsafe person in town was my Dad, who was infamously known, camouflaged by his grandiose confidence, and firm handshake. Dad was the man who continually created a fun atmosphere for his family and friends, the man to lead so many in our town, and the man who could shift anyone's behavior or attitude for the better.

It's wild how things can change in one Moment. Everything that was going so well can erupt in the blink of an eye.

After my sister and I turned him in as a sex offender, my Dad became the one person to look out for; this man's actions divided our family, and shocked the community. My Dad was now that one person in town who everyone shook their fists at in anger, hatred, and rage, bringing shock and strained looks to once smiling, friendly faces.

It began with the massages. I was 9 years old when the massages started. He and I would be alone in my parents' bedroom. He always had his shirt off, and would be lying face down on the bed, a sheet covering his lower half. He would hand me baby oil or lotion. As I was directed, I would straddle him, sitting on his bed sheet covered butt, massaging his lower back. He had me use a massage tool, because my hands were so small. He would praise my massage technique, continually telling me I was gifted, perhaps good enough to become a masseuse when older. I was 10 years old, when the massages went in a completely different direction.

It was family movie night. We often had family movie night on Mondays or Fridays. We usually watched movies in the living room, but on this night we watched them in my parents' bedroom. My sister did not want to watch movies, because she wanted to enjoy the privacy of her newly created room in the basement. My brother watched the movie on the floor, and I lay between my parents. Everyone had fallen asleep except me fell. I could never stop watching a movie. I was the sort of kid who had to see the movie right to the end, until the screen went blue on the television. I remember the screen turning blue, the blaring white noise, and wondering if I should turn the television off, or go to sleep. Above the sound of white noise from the television, I heard Mom snoring, deep and sound asleep. The quiet floor told me my brother was asleep as well. As for Dad, his body was shifting and squirming, letting me know he wasn't asleep. About the time I decided to turn towards Mom and go to sleep myself, suddenly I felt my Dad's hand on my thigh. I knew it was my Dad, but I thought that he might have mistaken me for my Mom.

Let It Matter

Walking tall
Feeling small
Smiling still
Heartbeat is paced to numb your fingers
Suppress.

Get home
Slam doors
breathing heavy
fingers cramping
collapse

Something happened
Something hurt
Feel better soon
Let it matter now

If you're bleeding
Barely breathing
Let it matter
It's the start of your revival
Your precious time to heal

first chapter

10 ON PELICAN AVENUE

Somewhere between misunderstanding and knowing, even as a child, I knew there was a better representation of love and happiness, than what I'd experienced. My life was extraordinary. Up until the time I was abused, my life was at its peak in peace. Everything was easy. I could breathe without worry or anxiety. I could find gratitude in all things I had. This became harder as abuse happened.

We were not a family of wealth, but we were comfortable. I'd sit on top of our swing set, watching life happen all around me. I simply sat up there to take it all in. To the left I could see a fire pit, the outhouse, two sheds that contained four-wheelers, snowmobiles, dirt bikes, jet skis, and a speedboat. To the right, a swinging rope hung from the tallest tree in our yard, the larger-than-life picnic table Dad built, a basketball court, the huge wavy slide, and finally, Dad's shop down the hill was all in my view. On top of that swing set, I could rest and breathe, away from the busy chaos that surrounded my family's lifestyle, the mess of a life built on being more. I knew even then, that I'd rather feel immeasurably more, than to project myself as something greater than all others. A deep longing filled me when I sought after this seemingly random desire, to find the almost tangible presence in something greater. It was something more meaningful than a career, or popularity platform. I didn't know what it was, but I had a strong feeling inside, maybe it was God. I remember firetrucks racing down the street following house fires. This feeling was thicker than the smoke filling the sky. All I knew was that it was real, somebody was with me.

From the top of that swing set, I'd pray as firetrucks and ambulances rushed to the scene of house fires. Then I'd pray, without ever being taught how, for their safety and peace, before returning to playing or daydreaming. Of course, eventually I'd return back to reality at home and carry on.

Even though this strong feeling I had inside me was almost tangible, in the end, I understood that my family was what I had and that this lifestyle is what I was given. My presence was required.

I grew up in this lifestyle with our ducks in a row. Each bird had its own personality. My brother, sister and I were all different types of birds. Dad was the Drake; the outgoing leader with grandiose confidence and a firm handshake. He was a businessman and an artist, always wearing a party hat as the most child-like facilitator of fun. Mom, the hen, wore many mantles herself: an excellent nurse and caregiver; a home chef always cooking something in the kitchen; and a spic-and-span hospitable hostess who always ensured a good time. As the heads of our nest, my parents were the town's charismatic couple who everyone adored, envied, and were attracted to, no matter the age.

My older sister was a golden pheasant — colorful, beautiful, calm and loyal. However, she could come across as intimidating: she was strong, held her own, fiercely defended those she held dearest, and was determined to seek justice in all things. She was the toughest, strongest bird of all.

My younger brother was the baby duckling, a real cutie! He had girls crushing on him, was loyal to his friends and loved hosting people at our house. However, he always wanted to be something greater. Belittled by Dad, he was constantly reminded that he was the youngest, the shortest, the most stupid and not a girl. As such, he became quiet, reserved, adaptable, and always lived in the present.

Me? I'm the bird in the middle. A vulnerable, ugly duckling. I am in the process of becoming a pen...a graceful, female swan.

FORGIVENESS CAN RESTORE YOUR
PEACE AND REMOVE A VICTIM MENTALITY.
FORGIVENESS CAN ALSO SET YOUR
OFFENDER ON A NEW PATH, CALLED THEIR
SECOND CHANCE. FORGIVENESS IS FOR YOU
AND CAN BE FOR YOUR OFFENDER TOO.

First Chapter

Imagine it. You're ten-years-old. You have lived a life built on fun, laughter, and jokes. Your only responsibilities are to honor your parents, brush your teeth and, have the best manners at all times. Then, all sound is silenced and that silence lasts sixty-seconds before it becomes a place, the loudest and most terrifying place you've ever been. What did you do wrong? How did you make him mess up? He probably thought you were his wife. You never slept in your parent's bed before. It was an accident. He won't remember. You were in the wrong place at the wrong time and it's your fault. If you say a word to anyone, you've ruined your entire family. He didn't just touch you inappropriately, did he? The back massages he encouraged you to give him before are now irrelevant. You have nothing to stand on right now. He is your Dad, you can trust him. He did nothing wrong. You have to figure this out alone. You are alone. Alone in that bathroom, you've locked yourself in to make sense of this. It won't make sense! It will never make sense! You will have to work through it alone. You're alone in this!

Don't tell anyone.

That silence was so loud, the only way to numb it was to obey it. Pretending nothing happened, while you're reminded that it did. Sitting in the living room with him on the couch, he suddenly recalls the movie night in Mommy and Daddy's room. He says it was such fun and wants to do it again sometime.Your quiet and feel speechless. He tells you to stop staring at him. Hone in on the television again and restart the numbing process. Bible Camp is around the corner, you'll soon have a week of distractions. He calls the camp to check on you, you refuse the phone call and play with your friends instead. Tell him, "I'll see him after camp!" In reality, I was living in a Moment where the nightmare didn't exist, and I only wanted to stay there a bit longer.

Silence can be the loudest thing. It's no wonder my Father always played music. Maybe he couldn't stand silence. He never was one to concentrate on any one thing. His biggest secrets were the talk of the courts after I finally had reason enough to speak up. I wasn't alone. My big, tough sister wasn't alone either. There was so much more to be revealed as my parents divorced.

There was a bar in the basement of our home. My Dad threw a lot of parties. He hosted neighbors, family and their guests. They really thought my family was the best, until things noticeably fell apart. Dad's parties were now so often, that sometimes Dad didn't even stay for the end. He needed hype and adrenaline to make him happy, and when that started wearing off at the party, Dad disappeared. Things were changing around the neighborhood. Our neighbors built a new house and moved near to the lake, and the parties became more frequent. Strangers were invited by their friends who invited even more strangers.

Mom didn't go to the bar in the basement much anymore, she'd just go to bed. Sometimes, I didn't know where anyone was. I was too busy pretending with my siblings that everything was all right. We were busy pretending there weren't teachers partying in the basement, porn playing on the television before our sleeping guests, with their hands not down their pants, girls cuddling girls, all while Mom and Dad slept with their door shut. My siblings and I had to keep quiet about everything and keep pretending.

School had finally started, and due to my parent's parties, it was up to us to wake up and get to the bus. Otherwise, we would be late and miss school. Walking from our bedroom upstairs, we tried to be quiet as a mouse while getting ready. I pretended I had not just seen porn playing on the television, but instead focused on my pink Bubble Gum toothpaste in the bathroom. Finally, brushing my hair and teeth, I'd dress and head out for the bus, where my pretending continued. "Dad didn't sleep with our neighbor that night. It was just a rumor." The only person I learned to carry my world was absent-minded, and Mom continually numbed herself in different ways.

I remember a neighbor saying we were going to live with their family for a bit. That was later on, because my Mom was admitted to the rehab center. My Dad admitted her, and in hindsight, I believe he could have done this to promote favor for a later custody battle. By admitting my Mom to rehab, he'd have the upper-hand, as someone having the initial divorce talk with my siblings and I. He'd have us on his side and was working to have everyone else on his side, but lies and slander will always reveal themselves.

When they discussed divorce, I already felt it coming. I saw my parents fighting. I watched as they distanced themselves from one another. I recognized my fear of Dad, and everyone's growing discomfort with him. Divorce was coming, and I already knew it. My Dad is the one who broke the news to us.

He carried on to tell us how he would redesign our bedrooms as we wished, bribing us to stay with him the majority of the time. Oh, the toys we could have! After my parents' separation, we had one of our first visits to Dad's house. The only decorating he did was concerning. He had painted his bedroom totally black, with a large, yellow smiley face on the ceiling above an awkward text that said, "Have a good day." It was obvious that he was desperate to come out of a mental struggle.

Oftentimes, he would tell us of his dream. He called them dreams, and I knew them as nightmares. To say the least, he dreamt up a life without Mom and my little brother. It hurt and confused me. Why was he so protective over my sister's computer and who she talked to? Why was he so protective and then theatrical with how he grieved the issues going on?

Once, January 5th, I must have been 13, he came to Mom's apartment. The three of us stayed with Mom more than Dad. He didn't understand why and hated it. We were to enjoy dinner together at one of his favorite restaurants for his birthday. My Dad was upset that his favorite restaurant was closed and that we'd have to come up with a Plan B. Rather than problem solving and figuring out another place to eat, my Dad sent us on a chase. We found him on some old and haunted trails, lying down in a cemetery. He lay on the dirt ground as if he were in a

Shakespeare Play, with an arrow wedged between his bicep and rib. He dramatically removed the arrow from the soil, and began speaking in a strange tongue, like a drunken pirate (similar to Johnny Depp's voice in "Pirates of the Caribbean" movie). He mumbled things to my Mom. My siblings and I made it back to the car, where we could tune out the sounds of their yelling and crying. Then, Dad joined us in the car taking the driver's seat and drove us back to Mom's apartment. It was a quiet, uncomfortable ride. Once we got home, my Mom tried to play peacemaker. We (kids) were going up to the apartment to pack our bags to sleep over at Dad's for his birthday. No one wanted to go. It became very evident once my sister yelled, "One thing! I could say one thing to put you away in prison forever!" His hand quickly flared up to hit her. I grabbed him by the wrist and he dropped the idea. Mom became hysterical, wondering what she meant by this. We (kids) went up to the apartment, where we pretended to pack clothes. The very moment my sister said she could put him away to prison, I finally knew I was not alone. She'd been abused too.

We made it back to the car again, where yelling, screaming, crying, and silence started to sound like white noise, until my sister yelled once again, "I could say one thing to put you away forever!" Again, his hand reached back to hit her, or I assumed, so I again grabbed him by the wrist a second time and his hand fell in his lap. I knew. He knew. My sister finally broke the silence. I wasn't alone in this anymore.

My sister and I were alone in our room. I looked at her while she avoided eye contact with me. I asked what she meant by, "I could say one thing...". Although I already knew in my heart, she wouldn't tell me, so I decided to tell her what happened to me. Then she made eye contact with me, though still quiet. I told her we needed to say something and she said no. I understood why.... he could have done worse to my sister; even more! My sister seemed fear based because of my Dad's threats and dreams. It came back to my decision to tell someone what happened to me.

Many believe that if they turn in something as hard as someone else's wrongs, that their life will be ruined. I know now that this isn't true, but at the time, I believed I could ruin my family by telling someone what happened.

My world stopped. My academics were on the back burner. I froze and knew I must quit pretending. I thought to myself, "Congratulations, once you tell, you'll have single handedly ruined your entire family."

The little girl in me grew up immediately to stand as a father and mother over her own life. My ability to dream was once fearless and limitless and now bound by fear and worry. Now, I felt I needed to walk around quietly, wearing baggy protective clothing, hiding any femininity, making eye contact with no one of authority...they could not be trusted. No one could be trusted in my opinion. If the people who brought me into this world had the power to remove my ability to trust their best intentions for me, how could anyone else keep trust in my relationship with them? My hope was destroyed. I was mortified, frozen and feeling hopeless.

MISCONCEPTIONS OF FORGIVENESS

- We think we can forgive only when the offense no longer hurts

- Forgiveness is not indifferenct about injustice

- Forgiveness is not a sign of wekness

- Forgiveness isn't saying "what you did was okay." It's saying the consequences of your behavior belong to God, not me

- Forgiveness is not accusing a person or letting them off the hook

- We think we must wait for an apology

- Forgiveness does not dismiss or minimize an event or situation

- Forgiveness is not indifferent about injustince

- We think we must meet face-to-face or resume the relationship

- We think vengeance is easier to carry.

- We're affraid we won't be able to forget the offense.

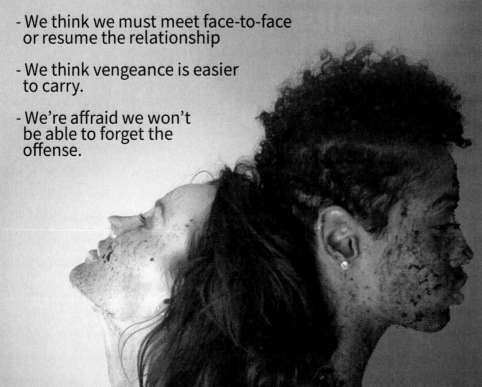

<u>What Is Forgiveness To You?</u>

The Girl Who Cried Forgiveness

There are so many more details in my story. Someone had to admit things weren't okay at home, so I did. I'm forever grateful to my school counselor for how she handled my truth.

More secrets were discovered after admitting the abuse to school counselor, Sara.

I cannot prove everything that came up since then to be true on my own, but rumor has it that my Dad not only had cameras on the outside of our home but on the inside as well. We were always watched, as we showered, dressed, undressed, slept, flirted with boys over the landline phone, and talked to our friends through email.

The cameras outside made sense to me. Dad wanted to know when a customer was coming to his shop, so he could transition from his office space to workspace. Was he paranoid of who would come? Was he paranoid of getting caught?

Rumors spread like wildfire and I am unable to detect the real truth. It is true that he molested me, it is true that he was not a good husband and it is true that he was not a safe father. It is true that he had inappropriate conversations with my sister's friend in high school online. It is true that none of this was okay and I needed to tell my truth in order to escape such a harsh reality. The truth is based on experience and direct evidence. All else are rumors that are believable, but unreliable. We weren't there. We aren't him, and so my heart softens.

This is a situation we popularly place beneath the list of "Sins unredeemable or unforgivable". I am grateful to not believe that, not concerning sexual abuse or even murder. Everything is forgivable and everyone is deserving of redemption. Nevertheless, forgiveness must come with boundaries; this is what protects us and makes room for self-respect and teaches others to respect us.

Years passed by so quickly. You will learn more about my story in full in future chapters as the time frame unfolds. However, to keep focused on my Father Story, let's jump ahead. I was 19 in 2010 and in Kansas City pursuing a one month long internship. I was having nightmares and flashbacks of the abuse. While worshiping in the ministry's 24/7 prayer room by morning, learning new perceptions and perspectives of the Bible and Jesus, I was also being opened to new belief systems regarding healing and forgiveness. During one night of worship, people were invited on stage to share their testimonies of being hurt, then finding restoration and healing.

I will never forget Chris Smith. In his dark biker-dude getup, with his silver mullet, Chris stepped on stage and shared pieces of the most vulnerable story I had ever heard on a church platform. Chris shared how he'd been imprisoned as a sex offender. He was now out and on this day, celebrating that he'd been forgiven by each person he'd violated. He looked free and liberated! The Christians applauded his courage, vulnerability and joy as I sat in shock. He then shared how he forgave himself and how this has completely changed his life!

It was overwhelming to hear someone who was in a situation like my Dad's, share with a sound mind that he had been forgiven and that he forgave himself. I imagined my Dad in Chris's place and on this stage with that microphone sounding over the church's web-stream and TV channel.

It was difficult because he was not my Dad. That was not my reality with my Dad and so it was just hard because I wasn't sure that could ever happen for him. I needed to hear more of Chris's story to keep in this fantasy, that it could be for my Dad, and just how forgiveness worked for this man. I'm confident this is my first introduction to the power of forgiveness. I needed to know more.

I walked to the back of the church and sat down. I needed to breathe. For me, this way of thinking was definitely a challenge, a different mindset, leaving me with quite a lot to internalize and digest. I couldn't sit too long as I felt squirmy, so I stood up and walked outside to pace back and forth in the parking lot. My Dad was on my mind. I wanted that freedom for him. I wanted that joy for him! I wanted him to feel the way I chose to remember him: creative, joyful, childlike, the facilitator of fun, kind, hospitable and present, instead of absent and not in my life. What if this forgiveness is what could provide that restoration for him?

Many believe that forgiveness is solely for you. I agree that it has changed my life completely, but I did not pursue the process. Forgiveness requires thinking of myself and my offenders and how free they could feel and how liberated that would make me! These people who were acting monstrous and caged by personality disorders, or maybe were conditioned to act in such grotesque ways could be free from those chains society decides would be there eternally, then I'd feel free as well. To see their freedom could birth my own.

I had to know more of Chris' story. I had to talk with my Dad. While pacing in the parking lot I made that decision. With my hands shaking and my thoughts racing, I dialed my Grandparent's phone number for the first time and asked for their son's address so that I could begin writing to him about forgiveness.

My Grandparents, aunts, uncles and I stopped talking almost immediately after turning my Dad into the authorities. They did not know what to do, embrace protection over their grandkids, or hold onto the shock and disbelief that their own son. After all, how could they ever believe the son they brought into the world , raised to be good, would or could ever commit sexual offense against his own daughters.

We just stopped talking because it was too overwhelming. It caused everyone to freeze in their tracks. Like the 7 steps of grief, we all lost what was wholeness. We were all in shock, denial, then anger. That is where it stood between my Grandparents and me for several years. This was the first time I'd even talked with my Grandparents in months since my Dad's sentencing. We were all shocked to hear one another's voice, let alone the words coming from my mouth. I then proceeded back into the building to find Chris and ask him to go out for coffee. I was afraid. I'd been so afraid of men, particularly my Dad's age, for so long. In high school, I only dated guys either younger than me or very slender. The age and body build made me feel like this person was incapable of hurting me like my Dad did. Now I was about to sit down with someone openly a sex offender and hear his story. I didn't expect this, but when I saw him, I hugged him and began weeping. This man was free!

We went to coffee soon after that Sunday and I grilled him with questions. I learned that he was groomed by his father on how to touch others. He was molested by his Dad in their basement and then began molesting the other kids in their cul-de-sac neighborhood. I learned that they hated him and once prosecuted, each one of his victims sent a letter in the mail to Chris. I think a couple of his victims must have understood the power in forgiveness and led the others to follow suit. These letters told Chris, "I forgive you for sexually abusing me." At this time, I could not yet fathom the idea of forgiveness. I could not grasp the energy and humility it would require for me to forgive my Dad and just how this could set him as free as Chris had seemed. I commend those who forgave Chris.

It is not easy, and forgiveness is not something that can be done quickly; it is a process. This process can bring up very challenging things along the way. Yet, they did choose to forgive him. Forgiveness is a choice. It seemed to set Chris free from his own haunting memories; I suddenly craved this for my Dad.

I learned that his own children did not know this about him and once he found value in honesty and transparency, he shared this with his children and they stopped talking with him. His sin was deemed unforgivable and he was not allowed to see his grandchildren.

The forgiveness that came from those he'd molested freed Chris up in a profound way. He was now able to see himself as a man, no longer a monster. As he regained self-worth, he remarried and was trusted to meet this woman's children and even grandchildren. Chris forgave himself and forgave his Dad and then was able to start over and live his best life. Chris died in a motorcycle accident in 2014 and I will never forget him and the impact he's had over my life.

At the time, I couldn't put into words what I was feeling. I just felt sure of what I needed to do, so I began writing to my Dad. I wrote the first letter while finishing up my internship in Kansas City. By the time I'd returned home to live with my Grandma, I sent the first letter, "I forgive you." I'd referred to him on a first name basis; calling him "Dad" wasn't possible without feeling confused and sick. I shared parts of Chris' story with my Dad, so he knew where this was coming from. I snuck the letter into the mailbox just before the postman came to my (Mom's Mom) Grandma's mailbox attached to the house right next to the back door. I had to sneak the letters in and out and I couldn't do this alone. My friend Dylan and I would meet at a coffee shop each time I'd get a letter. Dylan carried this burden with me. I kept this process from my family, simply because I didn't feel peace about sharing it with them yet. I did not feel peace, because I knew they did not agree with forgiving my Dad. It was very important for me to have Dylan, a supportive friend, involved in this process. Without him, the letters would have been too overwhelming to read and respond to all by myself.

You do not have to do these big things alone. Find your person. Dylan was mine.

I watched the mailbox like a hawk! Dylan lived next-door to my Grandma and me, so oftentimes we'd walk to the cafe together and he'd help me break the envelope's seal. He'd read the letter and help me decide if I should read it. I never knew if I could handle it, because my Dad's art work on the envelopes scared me most of the time. His drawings were new and unique, intimidating and sad. I'd bring my highlighter to these cafe letter readings. I'd highlight every manipulative word in pink then give most of my attention to that which wasn't highlighted. Sometimes this only left two paragraphs in a four page handwritten letter.

When I'd decided to move to Kansas City in 2012, I continued writing to my Dad. Though I couldn't always make sense of what he wrote or why he wrote it, I enjoyed having a father-figure back in my life.

This was a unique situation. I was hiding the fact that I was writing to him at all. I didn't want my family to find out, because I knew they wouldn't understand my heart posture. There had been so much division in my family. It was hard to watch as members of the family chose sides. I understood that for my family on my Mom's side, this act of forgiveness could resemble the act of acceptance and siding with my Dad. This is never what I intended. This is not my truth. Maybe it was the little girl in me, that I forgave him. I wanted to live in this beautiful world where he was good and where I wasn't fatherless.

Have you watched the movie "Saving Mr. Banks"? Have you seen the film "Walt Before Mickey"? Charlotteela Lyndon Travers wrote, "Mary Poppins" the book, as to remember her father in a way she wished to have lived with him before he died an alcoholic. Mary Poppins was her way of remembering the good about her father and keeping a hold of her innocence as a child rather than needing to grow up quickly to protect her depressed mother from suicide. She wrote this book to savor the positivity from her childhood. Walt Disney was not encouraged by his father. As an artist, most of his family called it out as "lame and non-profitable." Walt Disney did not have the best relationships with his Dad, but he loved him and through his animations and art, he was able to paint pictures that were reflective and healing for the relationships he wished he'd had. Sometimes, our fantasy worlds can be supportive of the future we desire to have. Sometimes, this dreaming will draw us closer to the life we ought to have. A simple life where we love and are loved rightly.

The things we fixate our focus on is what will build or destroy us. I decided not to fixate my focus solely on what I lacked but what I was going to gain. With that, my picture and memories of my Dad needed to shift. I needed to consider my childhood and remember what was good about my youth and my relationship with my Dad. I needed to forgive him.

I forgave my Dad for mistreating my mother. I forgave my Dad for molesting me and desiring to do it again. I forgave my Dad for mistreating my brother and my sister, lying to his siblings and parents and for not treating his personality disorders. I had to forgive my Dad for telling me his dreams of my Mom and brother dying so that he could live alone with my sister and me. I forgave his therapists for not working even harder to help him. I forgave my family and community for not recognizing what was wrong with my Dad and preventing such pain. It wasn't their responsibility.

I was able to forgive myself for believing that all he did was my fault. It was my fault for sleeping between my parents. I am not at fault for dividing the family, because I admitted the sexual abuse. I had believed it was my fault for every hardship my family had to grieve. When I forgave myself and forgave my Dad, mountains moved.

Time was nearing my Dad's prison discharge in 2015. He was about to be out of prison and on his 5 year parole. Throughout this time, my family had learned that I was writing to him and that I'd forgiven him. They'd learned that I was on the fence about seeing him again and they hated that I wished well for him. Still, I carried on.

I had moved back to Minnesota and was living with my Grandparent's neighbors. I couldn't bring myself to live with my Mom. At the time, I felt we clashed too much. I felt misunderstood; that what was good about me was only perceived as very bad betrayal. Mom and I grieved and responded to the situation very differently. We couldn't keep up with each other. I felt like by night, she was reverting as a teenager drinking late at night, acting like a grown up by day quick to keep her kids with her. It was unstable. I felt all stability was lost and she couldn't restore it on her own at the time. I know now she has her own story and has always had a right to process as she did, regardless to how we differed.

First Chapter

There was a time I wanted to be adopted. I told my friends that I didn't think I could have a good life due to the way my family was broken. My easy solution was adoption. If I could be with people who had less drama and abuse, my future might be a promising success, rather than stereotypical survival. I stayed with friends more than my Mom. I found adoption papers, learned of the steps I needed to take and asked my friend's Mom to sign it. I just wanted normalcy, joy, and stability back. I didn't have that with my Mom and her broken heart.

Mom was in shock when she learned that my Dad sexually abused my sister and me. Many thoughts were weaving in and out of her mind and heart, bringing unceasing, internal pain to her body. She thought, "How could I have not protected them or seen this coming?" The turbulence from the impact ricocheted, hitting so many members of her family. This was all so difficult to take in for our family. On top of a suicidal daughter with eating disorders, I was trying any way I could to get adopted by my friend's family. My desire to find normalcy and overcome my own pain divided her and me as she tried to overcome shock alone.

I worked at a boutique and a coffee shop at the time and as the date of Dad's prison release grew nearer, both jobs recognized that my head was not in the right place to carry out my responsibilities. I lost one job and fought to keep the other. Trying hard to act normal, I fought my own insecurities, brought on by triggers, flashbacks and never ending trauma, night after night after night.

No one knew how afraid I was that I might even pass my Dad on the road while driving. I played out multiple scenarios of him driving into my car, angry, crying, trying to get to me to hug me. My fears were shaking me to the core just thinking of his embrace. On the outside I forgave him. At this point, I thought I had fully forgiven him, yet the fear of the unknown was traumatizing. He was now a stranger with a strong familiarity. I knew of this stranger's past, filled with memories of absurd conversations about paranormal activity and things I'd rather forget, so I buried deep within.

One day, I went to visit my Grandparents. I trusted my Grandparents. Though my Dad lived next door to them and visited their home often, they always set a time for me to come over. I had one rule: I must enter the upstairs entrance, never through the main door downstairs. As usual, I entered the door I always walked through. There he was, as real as the blasting Tori Kelly songs in my ears. Ever so cautiously, I stopped, removed my headphones, and looked up to see him and said, "Oops".

I froze, in shock, still walking toward the stairs to run up to safety and familiarity with my Grandparents. My Dad was seated in the center of the long dinner table with a knife and fork bordering his juicy steak and vegetables. It was as though I walked in on his first good meal since prison food. He began to laugh and that laughter brought me peace. Without a word, he pointed for me to go upstairs and smiled. I went upstairs and told my Grandparents what happened and felt tired from the experience with my Dad.

My heart was racing. I was laughing with him nervously, because I didn't quite know what to say. I felt shocked. I was shaking like a leaf. I didn't tell anyone else that I saw him, because I felt protective over him since his parole. Though this made no sense, and I knew others would never understand my thought process, internally my feelings for his well-being were, as real as the abuse. Perhaps it was my desire to see my Dad have a second chance in life simply because he was my Dad. Like P.T. Travers, I longed to keep and protect the good memories so I could avoid drowning in harsh realities.

I wasn't naive to people's hatred of my Dad. Even those who were never directly affected by him or his offensive hand of abuse. Most of the town and surrounding community now saw my Dad as a detestable human being. People created false Facebook accounts in my Dad's name to project that he'd violated his parole. Others threw trash onto his driveway and yelled as they drove by. Facebook posts were filled with anger and hatred, while at the same time, these same people were trying to be kind to my family. "Don't worry. If I see him, I'll kill him. If he does anything out of line again, I'll hurt him!" These angry people, trying to be kind to my family, were starting to tick me off. This wasn't their story and they had not lived it, nor had they walked in our shoes.

I'd spent years trying to heal from this abuse. I spent even longer trying to heal my perception of all relationships, especially concerning fathers. I was there having to soak in the fact that he was out of prison, while I was suffering to keep my job, and to work through countless panic attacks. How would a stranger's vow to hurt my Dad help me?

Their seemingly good intentions did not not help at all, but rather made me all the more angry. Walking into my small hometown, heads would tilt with sympathy. How could their empathetic demeanor help me feel stronger, more victorious. It didn't and it never would. It only made me feel as the victim that they chose to see, not the forgiving overcomer I was choosing to be.

These well meaning people never realized that I had spent years healing, moving forward, growing in my own ability to trust again. As soon as my feet touched the soil of my hometown, it felt like time travel truly existed. Seeing these people and their pitiful looks towards me, once again, I felt pushed right back into feeling like that little, lost, innocent ten year old girl experiencing the abuse, trauma, and bitter memories from her past. This was a past where my family had endured many bitter memories, and one I was trying to forget. Why wouldn't they just let me move on?

To make my point for my Dad, my siblings, Mom and myself, even my Grandparents, I created a Facebook post to encourage other people in our community to move on as well and leave us alone. That post said something along the lines, "I've moved on. I've forgiven him. I have boundaries. I am safe. My family is safe.

If you have nothing to do with our family, please stop trying to protect us. Let us be. It is over. Let our family continue to heal. Let my Dad have his second chance."

My Dad chose to be nocturnal, reducing his chance of seeing people who felt it their job to bring him daily harassment. This was after he quit a welding job, where he'd been quickly promoted, after building a tiny home, and building up his new shop to host his auto body business. Being a relentless workaholic was something my Dad thrived on; his love of detailing cars and his tiny home gave him all he needed to succeed again. He was very good at what he did. Thriving off of detailing cars and living in a tiny home seemed to bring him the joy he needed to move on.

I had started talking with him some since I stopped writing to him through snail mail. Since he had been released on parole, I felt so torn. Deep inside I had a strong desire to show him love. I also wanted to respect my family and they're healing process. I knew I had to protect myself from feeling an overwhelming sympathy toward my Dad by setting boundaries. Yet, I wanted more than anything to talk with him, help and assure him (any myself) he wasn't a bad person; he was forgivable.

I stayed in contact with his parole officer and he walked me through the process of appropriately communicating with my Dad. My Dad and I exchanged a few text messages. Our conversations were merely random, surface, and light-hearted talk. We were strangers with so much history. Just as in his letters, I found I had to be careful of what he might say. Anything he said could be a trigger or open door to my past.

Due to the nature of his letters, I wasn't able to fully relax in my conversations with him. In light of my being older, I was still struggling with post trauma, listening to the parole officer's advice, and had many other concerns, too many to count. I think the most important thing that I was finally understanding though, was the realization that my Dad would never be the Father figure I wanted, needed, or longed for, no matter how hard I tried. Apparently, I was the one who needed to come to terms with this in order to believe it, although it had been reconfirmed to me many times over. I think there is always a longing and need in us to have a father and when we don't, there is a void.

As I started to see he was a self-centered narcissist, whose main desire was to please himself, I slowly started coming to the realization that our relationship as father-daughter could never be fully restored. "You cannot help someone unless they want help", and he didn't think he needed it. Everyone else knew he did.

It helped me to set healthy boundaries while studying at Avila University. I was taking a Personality Theories course. In this class, I began learning about personality disorders and how to properly and professionally diagnose them. This meant I needed to practice diagnosis in our final essay. My teacher approved my request to write about my Dad. This was a unique situation, and not one she usually approves of. With my forgiving nature and boundaries, she approved me to reach out to counselors and law officials from as far back as 2006 in my Dad's court hearings. She even approved of me reaching further back to some who had diagnosed my Dad much earlier. I researched personality disorders and recalled my Dad's behavior as a child, observed the relations, ideas and hard evidence of his abnormal behaviors from early childhood up until present.

When comparing his 2006 diagnosis to my diagnosis of him at the end of my paper, I found there wasn't much difference in either diagnosis. This pretty much summed up the conclusion of my paper, and in many ways, brought me peace.

I will not share which disorders I came up with, as people who know him and my family will read this book. I choose to respect his privacy for what remains private. I will tell you the results surprised me and provided me with much needed closure. I now have reason to understand why he sexually abused me. Yet I also wouldn't call him grotesque or perverse. There are psychological diagnoses that confirm to me that I did not deserve the abuse, nor was I responsible for it. My conclusion was that my Dad did not premeditate the abuse for multiple reasons, but I also concluded that I would never be able to have a healthy father-daughter relationship either. My diagnosis from his case study finally brought me closure and peace.

My boundaries now have become more defined since the case study. When considering my future, I now imagine one thing and that is my children. I forgave and still forgive my Dad. My boundaries now have become more defined since the case study. I have been able to escape a victims' mentality. I've been able to see my Dad in a different light, as a man who has been sick and might not ever seek the treatment he needs to get better. I do not feel it would be wise to connect my children with him in the future. One day, my kids will know the truth about him and I may need to help them in their process of forgiving my Dad as well.

When I forgave my Dad, I forgave the little girl who blamed herself for all he had done, as well as the consequences of his actions. When I forgave him, I was reconciled with the childlikeness in me and it revived my creativity and ability to dream again. Upon forgiving my Dad, he too was able to breathe again. My hope was that he would no longer feel like a monster, but like a man who did wrong, and is now able to do right by himself and others. Now, when I see reflections of my Dad in my looks, actions and mannerisms, I do not hate myself for it. I do not give extra time and energy to destroy that, but I acknowledge it and appreciate it. I remember beautiful Moments of laughter with my Dad, learning from him, and being encouraged to dream without limit! He once encouraged me, "If you can imagine it, then you can do it!" That was how I learned how to do a cartwheel, by tying myself to that belief system and by using my imagination.

My Dad's actions had countless consequences, affecting many people. Through forgiveness, I have been able to see myself apart from the abuse. Now I am able to look at my Dad through a different lens, seeing him without fear, feeling disgusted and gross, or afraid of being held captive. I can now even see other men his age, some who may favor him in appearance, and I do not see him; I do not quiver, but smile with relief. I now choose to believe there was some good in my Dad, like there is good in any person who's made a mistake (little and large). I also believe I inherited those qualities of his goodness, while still knowing I must always stand with my armor and boundaries intact.

I know it is up to me to protect myself, and those I love from the abuse I suffered, and his capability of abuse of myself or anyone else in my life in the future. I take this as my responsibility. Forgiveness doesn't mean someone earns our trust, but simply that we forgive and heal without disruption.

This is the power of forgiveness and the wisdom in boundaries; freedom.

Self-Forgiveness & Recieving Forgiveness

Forgiveness is: the only real path to freedom. To get free, you have to be very specific about what it is you're forgiving and why you need to forgive it.

When I forgave my dad, I also needed to forgive myself. I forgave my dad for becoming an unsafe person. I forgave him for no longer being the one person to example a good man. I needed to forgive him for every inappropriate word and act he pursued against myself and my family.

I needed to forgive myself for ever thinking it was my fault that I was in the way of my parents when I thought he acted accidentally. I needed to forgive myself for ever thinking a 10-year-old girl could ruin her entire family all by herself. This was powerful. Forgiving my dad did so much for me, like, making me feel compassion for this person rather than hatred toward someone I mentally dehumanized. Once I found perspective and compassion, he became a hurting person again and this took away all the energy I placed into hating him and pit-tying myself.

But have you ever received forgiveness? When someone forgives you, and you know you've done wrong or made a mistake, you lose weight. The weight of a burden you didn't feel you could shake; of an identity you felt was fixed on you each time this person saw you. Now, you can look at yourself with compassion and see a person again. You find freedom.

Do you need to forgive yourself? Are you able to receive their forgiveness?

Introducing The Forgiveness Letter

Directions:

BURN AFTER READING

Repeat as often as needed

ADDRESS TO SELF

Get in touch with this and really feel before writing.

Write about the wound, all of the judgement and fear. This part is not meant to be pretty. Write until it feels complete.

GRATITUDE

Now, write what you are grateful for in your life. It can pertain to this situation, or not. This prompt is meant to be the bridge from the wound unto forgiveness. Write until it feels complete.

FORGIVE WITH COMPASSION AND UNDERSTANDING FOR YOURSELF.

It is okay to be mistaken when willing to accept accountability. The compassion & understanding is the thing to give you access to forgiveness. Write until it feels complete.

DO NOT REREAD THE LETTER

This can erase the energy or harsh feelings you create as you write the letter through any doubt, questioning and judging of your words.

Resources and Therapies

PSYCHOTHERAPY:
Talk therapy using psychological methods rather than medical means

EMDR:
Eye movement desensitization and reprocessing therapy, most commonly used post-trauma

PLAY THERAPY:
Therapy that uses play to uncover and deal with psychological issues

> " IF IT CAN'T HEAL YOU, IF IT WON'T SAVE YOU OR THE OTHER PERSON, IF IT CAN'T MAKE YOU A GOOD PERSON (NOT ALL BY ITSELF), WHY FORGIVE? "

First Chapter

g u e s t   w r i t e r

SARA PENDER

Licensed School Counselor

I couldn't imagine my EMDR Superhero's any differently. The power of imagination is brilliant. What we fixate our focus on is what we will become. Through this therapy, I retrain my thoughts. If my mind is directed or swept up by the shadows, I imagine this team. The power of our imagination is wildly strong!

I've also created a metal storage container. In my mind's eye, I bolted this container shut with floating written words like, "Fear, worry, anxiety, lies, Jezebel, false sheep, unsupported, a dreamer and not a doer, etc." Now anytime more shadows attempt to bring in new written words, I have access to a vacuum that will suction these feelings into the storage container. They are gone and then I become invincible again.

The power of this is beyond me. I even felt a headache once I reached home from my appointment. The headache lingers today (the next day). I relate this to working out and feeling the throbbing of a muscle not stretched in too long. I have done work and it is good and helpful.

Our imagination is powerful. What we give our time and energy too is important. We can forgive people and experience freedom! Then what? We must then strive to find more peace by gathering our team of literal and imaginative support.

Honestly, I was terrified for a moment before my psychiatrist led me through my first EMDR session with him. I wasn't sure if I could relate what we were about to do with my imagination, to a positive or negative experience of mine.

Positive Experience: Grieving the loss of my best friend

was very hard. I hit the stages of grief and wasn't sure if I'd graduate any closer to functioning out of shock again. I went to a weekend seminar where people led "Encounter God Sessions" utilizing your imagination to connect with God in ways you haven't before. It was powerful, it was beautiful and good. Maria's husband shared just what happened the night she died by suicide. I am so visual that this memory has been locked in my mind's eye. As if I was right there with him as it happened, witnessing it and never able to unsee this. I wanted to remember our good times together laughing and making weird faces at each other while dancing to 13-year-old Justin Bieber love songs. In this session, I imagined myself with God and with Maria. I could see her smiling, childlike and happy in a new memory. This is my new default memory of Maria. I'm looking forward to how EMDR will desensitize the negative memory absolutely.

Negative Experience: I was engaged (that's a chapter in my book!) and it's a great thing that he and I are not married. More-so, due to the connections his family and I did not have together. We clashed on many things, especially how we connected with God. I went away to wedding plan and work without distraction of my then-finance. I went to Minnesota to be with family for three whole months! He and I thought we'd move to New Zealand and so this was quality time with my family before the big move. While I was away, I hardly heard from him. In hindsight, I see why. His mom google'd bullet points of Jezebel traits and was quick to decide I fit the list; that I was seductive, manipulative, controlling and more. When I returned to Kansas City, I thought I'd feel excited!

My body knew before my mind could process, that I was about to be in danger. As a collateral, I had to either experience Spiritual Warfare Healing Ministry, or I could not marry their son. I tried. What they did, was they brought me to the negative experience with my eyes wide open. The facilitator would look in my eyes searching. Always searching for the alleged Jezebel spirit residing in me. We made it all the way to the molestation before the facilitator called out Jezebel. I began to cry and was terrified! As if I was in that bed again feeling my dad's hand on my thigh, my thigh muscles twitched. I couldn't believe they thought this healthy and helpful. I had to get out no matter the cost.

Imagination is powerful. What we feed our minds; what we fixate our focus on is powerful.

Discover the type of therapy that is absolutely essential for our healing hearts and minds.

What support do you need? How will you have it? What does it look like? For me, I experience EMDR Therapy and it is highly effective.

"IF YOU DON'T KNOW WHAT HAPPENED YOU CAN'T KNOW WHAT TO FORGIVE."

What is Forgiveness?

You might be thinking you could never forgive a man for rape. You might think my story is powerful and will support others, but it couldn't possibly support you. If that is your attitude, you might be right about your ability to forgive.

My entire attitude and perception needed to shift before I was able to forgive the man who was meant to protect me from wrong. I was able to change my viewpoint when I chose to see him as the little boy who grew up and found influences to be stronger than himself. I was able to forgive. I was also able to remove the Stamp of "Victim Mentality" from my forehead. I then could see deeper into the root of the situation. He was a human after all, not a monster. He did do me wrong and I needed to move on; I needed to let go and in order to do this, I had to forgive him. I also had to find a way to forgive myself for ever taking the blame for things done to me.

See my photo pointing out misconceptions about forgiveness? Really, look deeply, look with your heart, soul, your entire being, because I want you to understand perhaps something you've never been able to perceive before.

Forgiveness is much bigger than the words we say. We can look like the most optimistic person in the world and yet hold unforgiveness, resentment and bitterness in our heart. Our actions will eventually play out, speaking louder than words. When we truly forgive, we become a force to be reckoned with, because forgiveness is a most-powerful tool to our freedom.

Forgiveness enables us to shed the weight of a burden brought about by pain and electrified by triggers. Forgiveness is like a computer reboot; restarting your internal way of thinking where everything is new again, your life is yours to control once more. You no longer feel under the control of others. The forgiveness process is simple, not easy, yet more than I expected.

Digging deeper than ever before, you tackle emotions triggered by your betrayer leaving all energy drained. You dig up all hidden pain and any remaining emotions left, lying cracked, broken, and in a million pieces, yet, you somehow manage to find forgiveness.

If you look at me now, you won't see a scratch, maybe you won't even see the scars, but my appearance won't tell you the whole story. After much trauma and by forgiveness, I am confident in this one thing, I am and will continue to heal.

Forgiveness, for all its value, cannot be offered by one person on behalf of the other. We might choose to offer forgiveness for the harm a person caused us. In other words, we might say something like, "On my child's behalf, I cannot forgive you for what you did to her; but I can forgive you for the pain you have caused me."

Forgiveness does set you free from the burden of a broken heart, whether you caused this brokenness or feel broken. Many desire to forgive and forget. That is such a popular yet passive process. I am not forgetting the pain. Hiding our pain, pushing it under the rug, suppressing memories, might seem helpful at the time, but long term, we will never resolve our problem this way. We only continue to project hurt and bitterness onto others in our life, until we finally choose to deal with the root, core issue of our problem.

The "fear of man" developed by molestation of my Dad could have forever scarred how I perceived men. With the feelings that came from being sexually abused, I feared those who looked like my abuser, or even had his mannerisms. This was the very thing that caused me to project unhealthy feelings into every potential healthy relationship with good men. I could completely sustain myself from male authority figures and write each one off as perverse. I could also subconsciously ruin all chances of a healthy romantic relationship due to my fear of intimacy while continually having my guard up so no one could take advantage of me. In order to move forward and have healthy relationships, I needed to forgive myself, as well as my offender, or my entire life, and all of my energy would be given to the one who stole much from me.

Since the dark secret was revealed, I now connected with people differently. Though connecting with women was easier than walking out my new habit to avoid men, I still felt unsteady around my female friends. I wanted to hide my body. I wanted assurance that no one would see my body image, or ever again take advantage of me again. I began feeding anorexia lies with layers of clothes, avoiding showing my skinny self to other girls. I was ashamed and afraid of my body.

I remember one school day sitting in English class, right before gym class, that I began to tremble in my seat. I knew we were going to the community pool that day in our bathing suits to practice swimming and gain points from the physical activity. All I could imagine was the layout of the community center.

The upstairs gym overlooked the pool through its large windows. I started imagining every man working out upstairs, all eyes on me, conceiving a plan to control me. Though this might sound far fetched to many, I wasn't able at that time to rationalize the truth. Truth from lies were all jumbled together in my mind creating an unreal thought life and world I couldn't seem to escape. I could only see and imagine conflict. I feared wearing a bathing suit so much for this very reason. The bell was about to ring, releasing me to gym class and I was still shaking.

I looked at my female English Teacher, and walked on. I picked up my pace and ran into the restroom to try and breathe before attempting to face the instructions my male gym teacher gave me.

Once the gym teacher wrapped up his instructions for the day, I began to panic. I felt this large elephant sitting on my chest and I didn't feel able to breathe or make one rational decision. I thought I needed to skip the class. I fantasized about running as far away from this feeling as possible. I ended up running back to my english teacher. I was shaking and she held me. I tried to explain just what I was feeling and that I hoped to be excused from this class. She would understand more than my gym teacher, he was a man. He wouldn't understand but only pity me, or so I thought. Thankfully, my english teacher walked me to my school counselor's office so I could talk my feelings out, and finally breathe again. My English teacher then spoke with my gym teacher and I was excused from the swimming segment of my gym class.

I had so much anxiety about that day in gym class. This unfounded fear carried over into my life as I projected it onto any male, everywhere. I questioned every man's motive. Who could I trust? Who would hurt me? Who was perverse? I needed to trust my male attorney, yet did this mean I needed to trust every male authority who was a part of the court house proceeding?

This process was a lot to handle for a young girl, balancing every feeble attempt to finish homework, avoiding the social awkwardness of life, all while internally processing everything in court. It was simply overwhelming. Now everyone in my small school knew about what had happened and how my family was divided. If they didn't hear it from the rumors at school, then by the local TV news or newspapers. Friends were being subpoenaed to court, a difficult process that no teenager should ever have to experience. Swearing into court under a sex offense case was too much. I felt so bad they had to come, and wished it would just all go away. However, in hindsight, I am so very grateful they chose to come. Their support is something for which I will always be thankful.

In between court hearings, family drama, and counseling sessions, I was busy trying to be a normal, undistracted, good student. It was difficult for me to do this, especially in my History class, where we were studying the courtroom and performing mock trials. This hit home for me and I was beginning to lose my cool about how seriously everyone was taking the assignment. This was my real world outside of school and now in school, for this class period, I could not escape it either. In the real courtroom, I needed to be adult-like, serious, and above all, honest. I needed to face the man who removed much of my innocence, as well as deal with difficult lawyers and questioning. In school, there were made up stories with added sarcasm. I couldn't handle it! "This is real life for some people! It's not some big joke! This is my life outside of school! You might have to go to court one day for real. At least you might be ready for it if you take this seriously!" I remember saying this before storming out of the class room leaving my friends to come to my defense.

What was that like? Heartbreaking, to say the least, for that class. I could not even slightly enjoy normal small talk from friend to friend regarding stupid things like boy talk, who wore what that day, music, television, or even simple book topics. I felt I had to grow up and deal with the hard things on my own, because no one else took it seriously.

I wasn't necessarily good at coping on my own very well. I was constantly overwhelmed just trying to enjoy the small things in life. I joined a local church youth group and spent much time goofing around with them. I spent as much time with friends as possible. While everything around me was invading all opportunities, I had to remain a child. The child within me kept fighting to be just that...a child. I had never been given any coping skills to get through this kind of trauma, so my half split adult/child persona was always at tug of war without me ever knowing what the outcome would be.

For this child, it was just trying to cope throughout my days, while everyone else involved fended for themselves. What does a half child, half adult who feels totally out of control resort to? For me, I gained a 4 year commitment with 2 friends, Ana (Anorexia) and Mia (Bulimia). I couldn't escape suicidal ideation. I feel I loved myself so much that I'd do anything to relieve myself from this pain. Without being taught healthy ways of coping or communicating through this, I internalized everything.

Sometimes I would go for a walk, and more often, I'd expressed myself in writing. Writing was my safe haven or safe place. In my journals, I could be as honest as I needed to be, as well as angry, frustrated, or confused. Through my journals, I could write whatever I felt like saying and no one could take these from me, for they were mine alone to express. With Ana and Mia, I had control over something. With everything else in my life slipping out of my hands, (family, friendships, and my social life,) at least I could control my weight. At this point I remember thinking, "I'd rather feel real physical pain than the emotional and mental drain that was dragging my life steadily down into the unknown".

I also spent a lot of time bathing. To this day, I take bubble baths when I need to decompress. I have more luxurious baths now than I did when I was fourteen. Then it was me and the water; my safe place to go to when I needed silence. Going beneath the water seeing nothing and hearing only the sounds of the water and the drain was all I felt I could do to drown out the madness. Underwater was the only place I felt I could breathe.

"Hold my breath until in Heaven I will hide." My Mom found this short writing crumpled beneath my bed. I wrote it while in my room literally holding my breath and imagining a beautiful place where adults didn't fight or do wrong things. In this place, people were playing and they were happy.

By the time I chose to breathe again, I felt a relief. My imagination brought me inner peace and the ability to choose when to breathe brought me a sense of control over what would happen in my life. When Mom found this writing she was deeply frightened. She knew to do nothing but bring it to our counselor.

REVELATION 12:11
They triumphed over him
by the blood of the Lamb
and by the word of their testimony;
they did not love their lives so much
as to shrink from death.

Post-sexual abuse, I felt afraid, like I was someone's else's poison. It seemed my duty to remove temptation for others. I wasn't prideful but insecure that my appearance would attract certain people to pedephelia. This didn't make sense to me so the only way to control this was by numbing my pain, gaining control over my body with eating disorders, and occasional promiscuity.

Now, I can finally say that what actually supported me throughout my healing process was my writing. While I am receiving the best therapy with a wonderful therapist I have connected with and fully trust, I feel I can now say this coming from a good place, that my writing will always be a tool that helps me through life's journey.

Types of Therapy

Psychotherapy	Talk therapy the use of psychological methods rather than medical means regarding mental health stability.
Psychodynamic Therapy	A form of depth psychology revealing the unconscious content of a client's psyche EX: In this therapy, a psychologist can discover why a client bites their nails. Perhaps it is underlying anxiety).
Group Therapy	Essential components addiction treatment therapy where you can learn skills needed to navigate through and from the addiction or grieving process (Alcoholics Anonymous, Anorexia and/or Bulimia Anonymous, Grief Groups, etc).
Art & Music Therapy	Creative techniques used to help people express themselves artistically, and examine the psychological emotional undertone in their art or music. These therapies also bring a sense of joy!
Solution-Focused Brief Therapy	Like positive psychology focuses on strengths rather than weaknesses, SBT places focus on a person's future circumstances and goals rather than past experiences. This is a goal oriented therapy. Any symptoms or issues bringing a person to therapy are typically not targeted.

Types of Therapy

EMDR	Eye movement desensitization and reprocessing (EMDR) is particularly for treating post-traumatic stress disorder (PTSD). PTSD often occurs after experiences such as military combat, physical assault, rape, or car accidents. EMDR is a method of reprocessing negative memories and desensitizing them so that you might be less triggered by that experience.
CBT	Cognitive behavioral therapy, or CBT, is a short-term therapy technique that can help people find new ways to behave by changing their thought patterns.
ESA	An emotional support animal (ESA), assistance animal, or support animal, is a companion animal that is intended to provide some benefit for a person disabled by a mental health condition or emotional disorder.
Psychiatry	Psychiatry is the branch of medicine focused on the diagnosis, treatment and prevention of mental, emotional and behavioral disorders.
Interpersonal Therapy	Interpersonal psychotherapy (IPT) is based on exploring issues in relationships with other people.

Types of Therapy

Family Therapy	Family therapy is a type of psychological counseling (psychotherapy) that can help family members improve communication and resolve conflicts. Family therapy is usually provided by a psychologist, clinical social worker or licensed therapist.
Play Therapy	A form of counseling or psychotherapy in which play is used as a means of helping children express or communicate their feelings.
Art Therapy	A form of psychotherapy involving the encouragement of free self-expression through painting, drawing, or modeling, used as a remedial activity or an aid to diagnosis.
Existential Therapy	Existential psychotherapy is a style of therapy that places emphasis on the human condition as a whole. Existential psychotherapy uses a positive approach that applauds human capacities and aspirations while simultaneously acknowledging human limitations.
Narrative Therapy	A method of therapy used to separate a person from their problem through writing stories.

Living the Dream

You've got it written on your face
All over your countenance I see it
But your words won't pronounce yet
Words describing the life you dream to replace
Every old habit,
Recall each planned scapegoat

We find you running
Far from where you are
So much past inside your present
Afraid of who you are
You can't cry, but you're emotional
So far replaced from who you are
Who are you?

second chapter
14 ON 4TH AVENUE

We can get lost in our circumstances as often as we find ourselves through them. Swept up in a flurry of confusion, sadness, anger, disappointment and disassociation, I could only escape through writing. I would write how I felt without a filter, without worry of anyone hearing and critiquing my thoughts.

On the pages of my journal, I could be completely honest and transparent. I could feel angry enough to cuss or doubt. On my own personal pages, I felt unapologetic. That all was to change for me the day Mom found my journal and turned it into a counselor.

The Girl Who Cried Forgiveness

It wasn't normal for my Mom and Aunt to treat just one child to pizza, still I was looking forward to a date with Mom and Auntie after school! They picked me up and we went on our way to GodFather's Pizza! We listened to all my favorite songs on the drive and so naturally, I felt very happy and special and was expecting quality time with the two of them. When we got out of the car, my family led me to a door beside the entrance to GodFather's Pizza. I was confused yet still followed suit. My stomach began to sink as I recognized the crumpled page in a counselor's office on her desk. The vibes I was getting from everyone were now somber and firm.

This was when I was shown the page and told I'd be going to a psychiatric facility. I'd stay as long as professionals thought I needed to be there. I couldn't hear anything else. I was internally processing again. I tuned their voices out as they looked at one another then looked at me.

I tried keeping my anger to myself because I knew I was stuck. I thought, "No one ever reads my journals. They haven't tried to learn the meaning behind my writing. I wasn't trying to plan for suicide, I was planning to regain control in my life. Suicidal ideation was real but passive. They didn't even know about the secret ease into eating disorders yet. Now, I have to go to a looney bin with a bunch of people with more problems than I actually have. So much for normalcy; there's no way to talk them out of this. I can tell. They've made up their minds."

I remained silent on my walk to the car from the counselor's office. I still felt stuck and angry. The only question they asked me was if I wrote what was on the page they gave to me. My facial expressions said it all: I'm stuck, I'm mad, I don't approve of this. Now, they would drive me to the hospital and turn me in.

Why didn't my counselor do her job and evaluate me? Why didn't she talk with me instead of my family? She listened to Mom to give her a response, not gain understanding from me. No one asked me what the poem meant! I began to cry.

Mom put on my favorite music, because she knew it would

bring me to a level of calm that I so needed. My knuckles were white from clenched fists and I began biting my cheeks before calming enough to sing the song, "My Jesus, My Savior" by Darlene Zschech. It was absolutely true that no one had understood me or had patience for me; only this invisible King.

We entered the hospital and I walked very slowly. I tried not to project how I really felt. If I showed that I was well behaved, perhaps they would see that I didn't belong here and decide not to check me in at all. I went in fully clothed as if going for a day of school, only to change into clothes without any strings or ties, plus the ugliest hospital booties. Everyone was assigned a room, a bed and a level. Your "level" declared how much privacy you were allowed or how much supervision was mandated for your case. The nurses took my vitals as I sat with the doctor who spoke broken, non-native English. I met my roommates in a thick windowed, plain bedroom. My roommate was on a level requiring more supervision than me. My window overlooked the skatepark across the parking lot. I watched as others my age had childlike, uninterrupted fun. In this glass house, I had to act perfect as if someone was always watching me. I didn't want to show that I had an eating disorder, afraid this might prolong my stay, but the food was so terrible, so after a short while, my two friends Ana and Mia (Anorexia and Bulimia) won. The battle and my secret was revealed.

I needed my parents to be okay. I needed a consistent counselor to be patient with me. This hospital was meant to be a safe place to feel, heal from eating disorders, and finally deal with this suicidal ideation I had.

This form of therapy was not helping me. I was distracted. I was surrounded by roommates who made me feel uncomfortable. In this hospital, I was mostly silent. In my room, one roommate watched me as I slept and woke up, telling me how much she loved me, and that we should run away together. Meanwhile, the second roommate was always trying to sharpen her toothbrush for self-harm. What made up the personality, and discomfort in this space were the characters of the people that surrounded me.

The only sort of therapy we had was a joke to me. Daily, we had our vitals taken, played some board games, had other supporting activities, all the while taking breaks in the hospital chapel.

I was just a person that was sexually abused. While this wasn't a matter to be taken lightly, it wasn't like I was crazy. I didn't need a straight jacket. I wasn't talking to myself, causing fights or disturbing others, so why was I here? My whole life was interrupted, and here of all places, all I was told to do to recieve help was to simply eat a piece of chocolate, like it truly was a "Dove " sent by the Holy Spirit. Yes, I'm making light of my situation, but these well meaning people through their good intentions, were only igniting a fire of rebellion in my tiny heart that was becoming too large to contain. I only felt disdain by the good that was meant to occur.

Was this chocolate really meant to teach me to savor the Moment? All I knew was I wanted the hell out of these savoring Moments. They did nothing for me but make me more bitter and sarcastic. I needed someone to talk with me, tell me I wasn't alone, look me in the eyes and say everything would be okay again. The thing I didn't need to hear was, "Now, allow this wonderful piece of chocolate to melt in your mouth and as it does, savor the taste. Remember to savor each Moment in life the same way." Nobody in the room cared about that damn piece of chocolate, and I'm pretty sure they knew it. We only wanted to be heard and understood. We needed empathy and a plan of action, in order to move forward, live and survive in this big world.

Instead of getting the help I needed, they continued taking my vitals, moving me from floor to floor to find a better fit, plus many other stupid, mindless things they called therapy, too many to count, none worth mentioning. I believe they had good intentions, thinking the longer I stayed, the sooner I would express my feelings and be ready for the discharge they felt right for me. Even at my young age, I knew I'd never be able to express my feelings to a doctor who was fluent in Mandarin, not English. I felt I landed in the twilight zone and my stay in this place was in no way supportive. Sometimes healing for myself seemed so far away, and out of my reach. I wondered if I'd ever be whole again.

I can get along well with pretty much anyone and adapt just about anywhere. One day I was writing my name with a marker and plain paper. This guy came up to me and told me he was going to call me "Ping". He didn't explain why, so I just accepted it. He then handed me a new sheet of paper and three markers. "I'm going to teach you how to draw flames, Ping!" he said. I smiled and allowed him to carry on. This was the most sane interaction I had with anyone so far. I would take most of my phone calls over lunch and avoid eating until they called for me to come to the phone. This same boy was my background music as he pounded on the walls and screamed continually. He'd been there for 3 days. He began his stay in the padded room, screaming and yelling day and night. I was told he was experiencing drug withdrawals. I also learned to tune that out. It's wild how someone acting so insane could make me feel so normal and at peace.

I had to learn to adapt to my new surroundings, feeling hopeless about an early discharge, due to the circumstances of my foriegn Doctor and our lack of communication.

I had visits from Mom and the youth pastor, who both gave me cards with many words of encouragement. My Dad's Mom even came! I was surprised and grateful for Grandma's visit. I thought she hated me for having my Dad prosecuted. My best friend, her Mom and sister came as well. In order for this to work, they had to pretend they were my Aunt and cousins. They took me for my first visit outside the hospital to Barnes and Noble and dinner out. I felt human again. I got to wear my shoes.

Just as I was adapting to my time spent doing lame activities meant to help me, the nurses decided that I might be best helped on a lower level of the hospital with younger kids. After-all, I wasn't even 14 years old. Everyone on the upper floor was 14 and older. I was about to turn 14, but my small, thin frame and maturity was misleading to others. Wondering if there would be a change in my behavior and desire to talk with anyone, the decision was made and I was moved to the lower level floor.

"PEOPLE NEED PEOPLE.
ESPECIALLY WHEN
TRUSTING PEOPLE IS
DIFFICULT. "

Meaning to simply adapt; I felt I had to conform, that I needed to communicate with people more, just so they could see joy in me. One day I left very agitated from a meeting with my doctor, due to his broken English, and my inability to understand him. I was about to have my first night downstairs where they decided to move me. I woke up very late that night, disturbed. I heard panting; heavier and heavier breathing right above my head. I woke to a boy who'd come into my room from across the hall, just to find him masturbating at the head of my bed. I jumped straight up out of bed, walked right past this boy, running to my sleeping supervisors. With fisted white knuckles and a furrowed brow, shaking their shoulders, while yelling straight in their faces, *"You couldn't even do this one thing! You didn't even see it! He got out of bed and is masturbating right over me! No one will help me because you think I've gone mad! You're not doing your job! You can't even protect me right here, under your nose!"*

Honestly, I can't recall what happened after that. I just know that I was released not too much later and it was on Mother's Day.

When I arrived home, I felt my mother's joy in having me back. I also recognized that same, lingering, somber feeling. I remembered thinking, "we must be returning to our new normal." Time carried on, as did school, and that dark and gloomy feeling of grief began to dissipate.

Reflection: Who am I?

A common reason that many people resist or avoid change, even if it will improve their lives, is because the issue they are trying to address has become interwoven with their self- identity. This is the case especially if the issue at hand is painful. People become attached to their pain.

It becomes part of their story—what has gone wrong, what has been done to them, how they've been hurt—so much so that they think it is who they are. Notice how part of you resists letting go of the things that make you unhappy and the compulsion you have to think and talk about it. Isn't it funny how part of you gets a peculiar pleasure out of your pain?

If you hate your job, but you believe you are someone who never likes what they do for a living, you may find it difficult to find a new, more enjoyable job. You would have to give up your belief that you are someone who doesn't like work. If you are mistreated or abused by your significant other, but you believe you are someone who is always a victim, you may find it difficult to remove yourself from the relationship. You would have to give up your belief that you are a victim.

The Girl Who Cried Forgiveness

In what ways do you consider a "problem" to be part of your identity?

_____

_____

_____

Do you talk about it alot?

_____

_____

_____

Do you get attention because of it?

_____

_____

_____

Does it give you a sense of purpose?

_____

_____

_____

You are NOT:
What you do
What you have
Your past
Your problems
What others think of you

If you find that your problems, pain, or the things you are discontent with are part of your identity, ask yourself, "is this who I want to be?"

The 3 Detrimental Identities:
illness, victim, poverty

Which, if any, of these are a part of your identity?

_____

_____

_____

What positive identy can you replace it with?

_____

_____

_____

The 5 Successful Identities:
grateful, engaged, forgiving, contributing, purposeful

How can you increase your identification with these qualities (statements and actions you can make)?

_____

_____

_____

_____

Confidence is Familiarity

The more time spent with something or someone, the more familiar you become. As you grow familiar you might feel confident about it.

When I studied as an Esthetician, I became familiar with the largest organ of the body: skin. The more time spent in a spa practicing facials and skin treatments, the more confident I felt about my ability to heal one's skin concerns while prescribing skin care regimes.

I was promoted as Lead Esthetician quickly. I grew confident after becoming familiar with my trade and the in's and outs of it.

Confidence does not come from the things you own, the space you live in or the car you drive. Confidence does not come from what you wear. Confidence comes from within and by familiarity. It comes from what you know and by application.

What do you know about yourself and your aspirations in life? What do you know about your purpose? Perhaps, if we spent more time becoming familiar with ourselves, we would not even crave confidence by acceptance of others. We would not require the approval of others because it will become enough for us to know ourselves; our truest identity.

The Girl Who Cried Forgiveness

How can you trust others after those you trusted by default filled your life with empty promises, stress and trauma? You absolutely can't. To trust people across the board can easily become like charcoal; a black spot on your life. I was expected to trust psychologists after other professionals placed me in a space that did more damage than good.

How could I practice honesty, while I had trust concerns? If I am honest, someone may misinterpret me, deciding I am unsafe, not spiritually saved or that something else is wrong with me.

Finally, I decided it was time to trust myself regardless of other's opinions. I knew where I stood. Ideas so often change in a heartbeat. From my own experience, I know I have learned much from mistakes I made. Do not fear starting over again. This time you are not starting from scratch, you are starting from experience.

I finally made the decision to take ownership of myself. Others may have encouraged me to do this in their own way, but I had to believe I could take charge of my life. To fully receive the support I needed, I had to let go of my victim mentality.

Another thing that's meant to be easy by default is breathing. I couldn't do that as easily as others because my lack of trust was replaced by a smoke screen of anxiety, taking my breath away during each storm.

Frustration existed because of my lack of trust, however, it also fueled my own personal coping abilities, bringing me to a place of trusting myself. By that time I was able to find more independence and grace for myself. I gained new confidence.

I learned that not everyone needs to approve, or even know of my process with decision making and how to learn from mistakes. During this time in my life, I watched many movies to keep my focus on other's experiences, rather. I observed these movies and played out how to respond to like-situations rather than fixating on my own.

Being honest and transparent doesn't scare me. I'm

unapologetic and fearless in thought about the things that matter most to me. I know my words matter and are meant to tell others whether I'm happy, sad, or scared. Someone needs to hear what I have to say, because someone else is experiencing similar hardships.

I won't pretend I'm the only person who has ever been sexually abused by their Dad, spent time struggling with suicidal ideation or eating disorders. I won't be ashamed because I know I'm not the only person who has gone to a psych ward when it wasn't good for them.

No chains. Just you

Vengeance is not freedom but a prison. When we choose vengeance, we're signing a blood oath to be chained to our enemies for the rest of time!

I had to compartmentalize what happened to me. If I understood my scars, then I could begin to forgive.

I felt ANGER. That's a part of the process so you are allowed to feel it! It is way easier to take all the that emotion and channel it into rage at another person. Do it! Anger is the fire that cauterizes our wounds to let them scar over and heal. Too much anger and you'll get third degree burns. Without a little heat, you'll never scar over and you'll never understand what happened to you.

guest writer

TERESA MCCLAIN

Psychology Professor

Teresa is a Registered Nurse, Psychotherapist and Sexual Assault Nurse Examiner. She currently consults, writes and teaches. Reflecting on her many roles in the field she says-

"These roles have given me the opportunity and honor of providing a variety of educational and supportive resources throughout our community."

When I met Vivia, the first thing that stood out was her bubbly spirit and optimistic nature. She came across as determined, passionate, and unstoppable! When faced with roadblocks and obstacles, she seems to have a natural ability to appropriately vent, then dive right into problem solving to find viable solutions. She tends to make lemons into lovely lemonade spritzers!

Vivia truly has an entrepreneurial spirit. She is able to build one idea into another creating a beautiful mosaic of resources. Despite the incredible adversity she's experienced, her ability to engage people and allow them to shine beside, not beneath or behind her, is a blessing and a true gift. She is courageously using her broken past, to rewrite a promising, bright future for herself, and those willing to take the journey with her.

I've had the pleasure of working with Vivia in many of my Psychology courses. One critical concept that we discuss often, is that anyone wanting to pursue a career in psychology must first work to gain as much knowledge and self awareness as possible before entering the field. A good psychologist must know themselves first; only then are they able to successfully help others. If they are unaware, or have their own unresolved issues, they will more than likely run into situations that result in frustration and ineffective client interactions.

We all have past issues, but they don't have to be deterrents or stumbling blocks interfering with our ability to help others. Like feelings; feelings aren't right or wrong; they just are. It's how we process and handle them that counts. As practitioners we can only lead a client as far down a dark path, as we've been willing to go for ourselves. To hold a lamp for someone else, you must first light it for yourself. Clients can often spot, and will develop distrust, for someone who just spouts psychobabble.

Potential practitioners also need to be acutely aware that this is not a "one solution fits all," career. Nor does it provide instant gratification. What one gives to clients in terms of time, guidance, and effort, is given with the client's needs and goals in mind. You are there to validate and assist the client, not the other way around. You may never see fruit from the tree you just watered, nurtured, and diligently supported. That can be a tough one! Rather, we hope that any assistance we've offered, kicks in to serve the client when they need it most. Skilled clinicians understand that if we do our best, it's up to the client to do the rest.

You'll find that most clients aren't interested in your pedigree. What they need, is to sense that you are able and willing to understand them right where they are. We don't condone maladaptive behavior. But we do need to be able to empathize, take the time to learn about where they are in their journey, and work with them to learn how to build skills and coping that will serve them better than what brings them to you in the first place. They need to know we are strong enough as a person, and knowledgeable enough as a professional, to help them.

A skilled practitioner treats each person as an individual. They do not refer to clients as a diagnosis or set of problems. The client may have already been pigeonholed by many practitioners before meeting you. They want to know if you will listen without judgment or making snap decisions about who they are and what they should be doing.

A good counselor spends time getting to know a client, before deciding which interventions or treatments might work. The client is an active participant in this process, not an observer or a test subject. The clinician needs to create and nurture a collaborative relationship. It's easy to focus on negatives, so it is vitally important to identify a client's strengths. It's also imperative to know the client's negative perceptions, behaviors, and coping mechanisms since what they've been doing so far has not worked.

In examining Vivia's experience, the psychiatrist she met at fourteen may have been more successful had she done things differently. Awareness and utilizing the elements of the client-professional relationship that have been discussed would have made the psychiatrist a better advocate for Vivia.

The ideal approach with any client, is to first sit down and have a dialogue about who they are and what brings them to you, before making any clinical decisions. Without more information, you simply cannot build trust, assign a diagnosis or prescribe meaningful interventions.

If psychiatric help is indicated, it is paramount to explain exactly what that intervention entails, and why it may work for them. This is especially true when working with adolescents. If no trust or understanding is established, you might as well throw your therapeutic plans out the window. It becomes your plan being forced onto a client who doesn't know you, let alone trust you. Not many of us would feel comfortable doing that!

In today's healthcare climate we don't always have as much time as we'd like, but we need to do the best we can with the time we get. In Vivia's case, the psychiatrist didn't know the details of her life or the intricacies of her problem. Due to this lack of insight, the clinician didn't have enough information to determine the best move to support or help Vivia.

If someone needs professional support, but has only had negative experiences with therapists, they will understandably be cautious about entering into yet another fruitless relationship with a helping professional. That is where the professional's motives and skill level are so critical. Helping clients to figure out what it is they really want, and then brainstorming with them to figure out how to get there should always be the number one goal. In one of my favorite films- the therapist asks the client why she finds herself in placement.

Client responds "you talked with my mother, didn't she tell you?"

The therapist responds- "yes, she told me what she knows, but not what you know. Only you can tell me that."

From the first encounter, trust is being established. The psychiatrist acknowledges the client's experiences as real and valid.

In Vivia's case, rather than automatically placing her into inpatient treatment, it would have been helpful to get to know her, then collaborate, discussing options to determine the best course of action. Vivia was not an active danger to herself or others, thus immediate placement was not automatically indicated.

When considering professional help, interview several practitioners. Most of the time your gut will give you a sense about whether that particular clinician might be right for you. Absolutely trust that feeling! Ask specific questions, be honest about what you're looking for. This process is a collaboration, versus looking for someone to tell you what to do. After all, it's your bicycle, your life. You are best qualified to eventually take the training wheels off and ride!

Finding Your Therapist

You might not always enjoy your therapy sessions. You might not always like going to the gym! Once you've done it, you'll likely recognize that having gone feels a lot better than "going".

It isn't uncommon for things to get worse before they get better, but when you put in this work, you will feel better long-term! I encourage you to push through this discomfort. I believe you will end up at a much clearer place.

Meeting with your therapist is not a life-long commitment. Feel free without places too much pressure on it to go perfectly or to stick with it if it wasn't a good fit. You might use one therapist once or twice before carrying on shopping and that is ok. Finding clarity is for you and facilitated by a therapist; you are the most important and need to find someone you connect with. I have seen multiple therapists. I connect with one therapist for advise, another for EMDR and another for anxiety.

What are your goals for therapy? If you're unsure, don't worry! A good therapist will help you figure them out. Whether you are wanting to find direction in your life or deal with anxiety, there is not one right reason to go to therapy.

Therapy is more-so about incremental steps toward a deeper understanding of yourself and your world than having a huge epiphany. Sometimes life requires a little untangling. Give yourself time.

There will be times you may not like your therapist. Even if they are the best! They will tell you things that you don't want to hear and challenge you to reflect on less-than-flattering things about yourself. This might result in you disliking or mistaking your therapist. This is normal!

When in therapy, you have entered into a place to practice for real life. Learn how to communicate, stand up for yourself, how to argue well, apologize, forgive, be vulnerable, etc. Challenge your therapist and practice with him or her admitting your faults out loud or voicing anger.

You can ask your therapist anything! You are allowed to ask whatever you want, so let your therapist explain their boundaries. A lot of the work actually happens outside of the therapy room and so asking questions during your session helps you to put what you've discussed during your session, into practice outside your session.

Journaling post-session is a good way to get the most out of therapy. Take notes after your session and write about what you covered, what things were hard to talk about and lessons or things to remember. You can also note the things you forgot to bring up or would like to revisit next time. It's even okay to write about what you wish to talk about before your session!

You do not have to be unwell to start therapy. It is not always a reaction to illness, but instead it can be an active engagement in wellness. Prevention is much easier than reaction, being in therapy will give you the tools to better your relationships and better deal with challenges when they come up.

When you're in a session, know you will benefit much from clearing out time around your session. Set your phone to do not disturb, tell anyone who might need you that you won't be available for a bit and avoid scheduling anything immediately after your appointment; you might find you need some time afterwords to decompress. Even thirty minutes can help!

Expect to talk about your history. The challenges we face now are invariably responses to something that happened in the past.

I Am Spring

I watched the ice split apart,
I knew how it felt.
I forgot that seasons change
that fresh water was the result.
Dead grass awaiting its awakening
to bring alive the land with its green.
The trees standing tall, more beautiful than last
Spring,
still feeling blessed with their surrounding scene.

An eagle lands on the third tree to my right,
It's eyes read my story.
I am Spring,
wherever I am,
I am renewed more day after day.
Where I am and where ever I will be,
as so do all things around me change, let it be
me.
I Am Spring.

third chapter

16 IN SUNSET HILLS

I'm sixteen now and living with my Mom. She bought a house in Sunset Hills, a development just five miles out of town. It is beautiful and I'm happy we can "start over" here. Now, at this season of my life, Dad, awaiting sentencing, remained in and out of county jail, due to his parents posting bail again after again. I'm not saying they made a bad choice, they were just trying to help their son. This in and out business was exhausting for everyone in our family, and no one knew quite how to respond to each other. He called Mom leaving more voicemail messages, but those slowly dissipated.

One morning, we got ready to leave for our family counseling session. My Mom was flustered because she hadn't heard from my sister all morning. She knew her tardiness would make us late for our counseling appointment. It didn't take long before we heard a knock on our door.

A police woman and a social worker appeared. They were on a mission, and quite direct in how they handled everything, making us feel very ill at ease. We were caught off guard, upset, scared, and confused. We didn't fully understand why they were telling us to pack our bags. Mom was hysterical and I became defiant at the intruding professionals, that came out of nowhere disrupting our home life.

I do not remember how my brother felt, and I don't know why, unless I was so focused on the entire situation as a whole. It was overwhelming, to say the least. My thoughts would be that my little brother became a wallflower at that Moment, fading into the background, hoping it would all go away. But, it didn't go away for any of us, and we would soon know why. As they encouraged me to pack, they reminded me to grab my toothbrush. I grabbed it alright! I threw it at the social worker and yelled, "Tell us what's going on! We need to know!"

As we walked to their car and away from Mom, I could feel this unspoken anger in my brother's silence. I kept asking the police woman and social worker questions, without getting any answers. Their unanswered questions only fueled my already inflamed emotional state.

When they finally told us where we were going, they still would not tell us why. They tried having small talk with us, but I kept asking for a reason, to no avail, getting nowhere with these people.

They took us to my Aunt's house. When I saw my sister there, something clicked, I knew there was a good reason we were taken from my Mom. We were then told we would be living there under the foster care system. Our separation from Mom would last for a long and horrible 8 months.

It took a while, but I finally learned that Mom had gone against our restraining order against Dad. My Dad thought if he talked with her while he was out on bail, he could convince her and she would finally see everything his way. He needed my Mom to then convince my sister, but he underestimated my sister. That was never going to happen.

Looking back, I now see how he was manipulating my Mom, but to get what he wanted, he needed her help. My Dad always found a way to manipulate others to get what he wanted, finding our weaknesses. My Mom was especially vulnerable to his tactics, because she loved him. I don't think my Mom thought that what she did was wrong, or even a non-compliant act, but we all paid the price for what she did. My Mom's non-compliant act, allowed my Dad to manipulate her as he did, causing havoc, frustration and finally, the ultimate wrong, separation of our already bruised family.

Perhaps my Mom had no idea just how much manipulation and control my Dad had over her. This is a very complicated situation, and many people find themselves living in these situations feeling they are normal, when they are anything but normal.

Here's how things went down; From the Moment my Mom agreed to visit my Dad, everything went wrong. Dad had a plan and Mom agreed to it.

Mom had taken my sister to practice for her driving permit. After Mom took the wheel back, she drove my sister to my Grandparent's house. Arriving in their driveway, there was my Dad, waiting for both of them. He got in the car. I was told he was very frustrated, and that he let them know just how he felt. He was trying to say that those things had not happened, and what the family needed to do was get back together. This was his solution to everything. Maybe he was so overwhelmed by the situation, that this was why he lifted his shirt to show my sister that he was armed with a gun.

This became a snowball effect, resulting in my sister telling my Aunt, my Aunt calling the authorities, the authorities calling Foster Care and Foster Care intervening. Foster Care arranged for us to live with my Aunt and her fiancé until such a time they deemed my mother a fit caretaker for us again.

For me, personally, I just wanted to understand why. Why did Dad act as he did? Even if he were the bad guy, it was still difficult to accept him as the enemy and I still wanted to understand him and know why he would do this to hurt my family and me. Why would he bring weapons into the situation? What was going on in his head? Did he really believe his actions would make him look as innocent as he said?

I was already in a state of anger, rage, confusion, shock, and even partial denial that this was actually happening to my family. On top of everything , I shouldered the blame myself, that I had ever brought the truth forth. What good was truth, when in the end, my family shattered into a million pieces. Now the Foster Care people's decision to take us from Mom only added more fuel to the already raging, burning fire in my life.

Families should do life together. Families should encourage one another. Families should cry and grieve together. My family became segregated, isolated, avoiding each other, and closed off to one another.

My sister was close to my Aunt's fiancé. I only had one relationship to relate my sister's relationships with a man, that was the relationship with her and my Dad. I felt sick when I saw the two of them talk. I was nervous that this man would hurt my sister as well. I did not spend much time building trust with this man, simply because he was a man. I wouldn't eat, I wasn't listening to what he and my aunt had to say about anything.

In my room, I was dealing with depression and crying alone, avoiding others' interactions as much as possible. I simply hated living so far out of town. I hated my life! I hated that I needed to ask friends to get background checks, in order to have slumber parties with me. I hated going to the same school where everyone knew what I was going through. There was no escape. I was always watching others and hearing the local town gossip surrounding our family. Normal wasn't possible for me anymore. I had no normalcy at this point in my life. The only thing I had in my life that brought any sort of joy was my Wednesday night youth group. My life became a routine of going to youth group, then spending time with my best friend and her family.

The Girl Who Cried Forgiveness

We were all upset with Mom. My siblings and I were on different pages regarding forgiveness. Meanwhile, I craved visits with Mom at "Positive Connections". Positive Connections is a business that offers supervised visits between parent/s and their children who have been taken from them by the state. Though we could not discuss anything actually going on (regarding our case), these visits brought me a sense of normalcy.

We were allowed no questions or answers from Mom. This was only a surface level conversation, but it was just what my heart needed. I think this was what my brother needed as well, because both of us jumped at any chance to meet Mom. My sister did not visit Mom. She remained distant and uninterested, perhaps because she didn't trust her or feel safe with her since the incident with Dad.

It did take my sister a while to forgive my Mom, but by this time, Mom had moved into a different home in a new city. My brother and I soon joined her and transferred schools. My sister lived with us too, but commuted to our original school. Even the counselor responsible for turning my Dad in after I confided to her, transferred schools with my brother and me. That brought me comfort that I had someone in this new place who knew me. I felt safe with her there.

Life was very different now. Mom was starting over, and it was apparent she wanted to develop a new life for us as well. I'm not sure we knew what to expect, or what normal even was, but she was trying, so we also tried. Changes went far beyond living in a new city. Besides our transferring schools, we also started going to church on Sundays, and eating meals together. Mom knew this change was necessary if she wanted to keep our family together.

I want to be sure you understand I do not blame my Mom for anything that happened to us. She did not know, and once she did, she took action the best way she knew how. She changed our lives for the better by inviting us to transfer schools, cities and church, even while dealing with her own personal world falling apart.

As a counselor, I now see the trauma she herself was experiencing, things she regretted, and things that grieved her. I felt my Mother did the very best she could do, and I applaud her for that.

Coupling her loss and pain over her marriage and family, along with her daughter's trauma, I cannot even fathom her thoughts, nor do I want to pretend to know what she walked through as a mother. Let's just say, I've come to a new appreciation of my Mother. I now see that while her world was falling apart, she was trying her best to hold all of us together as a family. That can never be easy, no matter who you are.

We went to our counseling sessions and learned to communicate with each other as a family, so we could start to thrive and grow. Naturally, my brother, sister and I didn't make this easy for Mom. I didn't want to go to the church she picked for us to attend. I wanted to go somewhere else, where I felt a sense of belonging and could have fun! The church she chose seemed stiff and rigid. I promised her I would go with her, until I got my driver's license. About the only thing we did agree on, was that it was nice to be in a new school. I could be Hannah Montana, having fun, exciting adventures without anyone knowing what happened to my family. I could be the teenager with new friends in school, the girl that everyone liked. I could have friends who didn't know about my Dad. I just needed to feel something, anything, that wasn't from my past. There was only one small problem. This image I was portraying was not totally the truth.

I could appear cool and collected at school, but outside of school, things were quite different. I led a totally different life. That life was one I could not escape. The past events would continue to tie me to my imprisoned father. While I hated everything that happened to me, my sister, our family, even then, something inside told me that telling others my story would somehow bring me the freedom I needed.

So, I started public speaking. I began speaking first at small and local events. This was one of the hardest things I'd ever done, facing the demons attached to my painful memories and haunting past.

It wasn't that I necessarily wanted to speak publicly. I never even had a desire for my story to be filmed for documentaries. This wasn't something I envisioned when starting to speak, but in reality, being in a small town gives you few options. I felt public speaking was like therapy, and if telling my story repetitively was my answer to healing and overcoming, so be it. I knew I could do it.

I had already received many therapy sessions that I did not find helpful. One counselor doodled on the pages of his clipboard the entire time. He lazily asked how I felt about what I just said, letting his clipboard lean heavily down his knee as he waited for my answer. He didn't even try to disguise his unprofessionalism or lack of interest.

Another counselor only asked how I felt about things repetitively. She was not helpful at all, never sharing any advice or perspectives on my situation. Rather she let me speak, watching as my head drooped down and my words fell to the ground. Another counselor met me only once, then sent me to a psychiatric ward without even asking many questions. She had already made the call to the hospital before I arrived, because Mom was frantic about my suicidal ideation.

"Hello? Anybody there? Talk with me, help me understand what I am going through." Perhaps if someone would communicate with me, I could finally start to understand and process all the things that happened to me, my sister, and my family. Each counselor just signed me off, handing me over yet again to another counselor. And so the saga continued, with each new counselor never gaining understanding of my problem, or even trying to have the slightest clue of what I had been through. I felt no one would ever be able to empathize with how I felt or how the horrible experience I went through affected me. It would just keep being a daily reminder to me that my life might never

return to normal, and that was the one thing I desired the most.

I began speech lessons with a group called ToastMasters. I shared my story at local churches, schools, and counselor's conventions. I received floral bouquets and large checks, in exchange for night terrors and wild flashbacks. I couldn't totally decide how I was to feel about this process. In any case, I wasn't avoiding my story. After all, it was my truth to tell, but I also did not want to become fixated on it either.

While attending the church Mom chose, I pursued a spot as the youngest member of the church council. This council had influence in making the decisions for the worship teams and mission trips. I went through Confirmation as well. Upon graduating from Confirmation, I shared my story for the first time. Everyone had to share their "faith impact story." I shared what had happened to my family and how my faith in God supported me during that tragic time.

Everyone had an icebreaker to ease the pressure of their first time public speaking. I was asked, "If you could have one thing, anything, what would it be?" I answered, "Braces! I am going to be famous one day and I'd like a pretty smile!" Someone, still anonymous, paid for my entire family's braces! After braces, my confidence soared! As my family and I allowed for time to heal us, our smiles grew wider. My smile has been my most complimented feature. As a new public figure, I will never forget my gratitude and will continue to care for this amazing gift.

The church was growing on me, yet, I wasn't satisfied. I was looking for a way out. I went on a mission trip to my favorite side of the US in Boston, Massachusetts! I developed a great friendship with a girl I went to school with and enjoyed singing with the church choir and worship team.

It was such a good trip. Something was wrong with how our team connected though, because I started receiving texts from an elderly gentleman who was on the trip, and also part of the council. This had to be a mistake. At first these messages seemed random, but it didn't take long for me to see they were premeditated and becoming fixated on me. He started out by inviting me on a mission trip to New Orleans, alone with him. I didn't understand this, and brushed it off. I told him I didn't want to go without my friends. He told me he'd keep me updated if anyone else were to join.

After it was evident no one else was going, he began leaving me unending voice messages. He told me he had to see me. He told me I could meet him at his workplace after he closed at 10 p.m. I was fifteen, had braces, an eyebrow ring, and my nose pierced. What was this 50-something year old divorced man's obsession with me?

The voicemails continued. I noticed he started watching me leave school when picking up his son. His messages became scarier as time went on. I did the only thing I knew to do, by sharing the voice mails and text messages with my school counselor who encouraged me to threaten a restraining order if his behavior continued. I informed those in authority at church, and I never heard from him again.

I was surprised the church did not take this news as seriously as they should have. They hesitantly talked to him and let him carry on as an active member in their church council, regardless of everything I showed them (my copies of his texts and voicemails).

" A SUPERMAN, OR SUPERHERO COMPLEX, IS AN UNHEALTHY SENSE OF RESPONSIBILITY. WITH THIS, ONE MIGHT BELIEVE THAT EVERYONE ELSE IS UNABLE TO SUCCESSFULLY PERFORM A TASK OR ANY ACTION. THIS PERSON MIGHT FEEL A CONSTANT NEED TO SAVE OTHER PEOPLE, AND IN THE PROCESS, TAKING ON MORE WORK ON THEIR OWN. **"**

Third Chapter

A Superhero complex is an unhealthy sense of responsibility. With this complex, you might believe that everyone else lacks the capacity to successfully perform. My friends call me *Mom* sometimes, because when they ask for advice I tell them the truth, and when they don't listen, I am always there picking up any pieces that are broken, trying my best to mend them together again.

I've also struggled with this weird idea that if I am as perfect as I can be, *then* I can be a better friend, sister, child, significant other, coach, etc. I tend to overthink everything I say, hoping I won't blow it with the people I love. I have to continually reassure myself that I can help the situation become better if I am honest. I can support others better if I leave them space to grow on their own. Their mistakes help me see the imperfect parts of my own life.

I was a victim. Now I am overcoming. I feel after turning my Dad in I gained a heightened sense of awareness and discernment. I knew I could make a difference when I saw people hurting and afraid. I knew without proper knowledge, training, and healing, I could not help others well enough. I didn't want to be responsible for putting any person I was trying to help, at risk. Hurting them would never be my intention, so I needed to make sure I was healing from my brokenness. In order to help others the way they needed to be helped, I wanted to know my heart was in the right place, and that I would never project my pain onto them.

I actually thought I was learning how to filter my desire to love people by looking at their hardships when they reached out for help. In retrospect, due to my own untended wounds, I had things all backwards and the cart before the horse, as they say. I did not need to be helping others. I still needed help myself, and I had not found the answers for that which I was seeking, but I knew someday I would.

There are many who carry compassion to support others. Their heart is right, but anything we do to lift ourselves first (before the person we seek to help) can cause severe consequences and backfire. Doing this can leave the person more wounded than they were in the beginning. I want to be honest about my opinion concerning Life Coaches. Unless your *Life Coach* has a background in Psychology, I suggest you avoid taking heed to their advice.

There is a common psychological phenomenon called the *"Barnum Effect"*. This is when individuals describe your personality in a way that is, in fact, vague and general enough to apply to a wide range of people. Life Coaches seemingly master the Barnum Effect, as well as psychics, horoscope writers, and even some false Christian prophets.

These services can come at a high price and don't actually deal with you personally and in a safe way. They could harm you, but as long as you are smiling at the end of a session, they feel they've done you right!

Here's an example: I know several Life Coaches who mean well, however, I will not refer to one person after hearing their motive. *"Don't fear my prices. You need to acknowledge your self worth. Once you know how much you are worth, spending a lot of money on coaching sessions, a car, the trip you want to take to Bali, won't scare you!"* So, this gets you in their back pocket. This does not show care or wisdom in counseling you. While they are motivating confidence, independence, freedom, and self worth, you could be drowning in debt and unable to breath from financial panic attacks, driving your depression deeper, and ultimately, (coming full circle now) making you feel stupid, inescure, and not worth a dime.

Those who study Psychology, learn how to support people not by telling them what to do or by hoaxing them, but by facilitating your thought process so that you can make a clear decision for your life. Psychologists learn how to support you after understanding more about you and your history. They take the time to assure their words only lift you up and help you to cope without codependency or the promise of a richer, grandiose life at the end of one session.

As a counselor myself, i.e. Clarity Coach (Life Coach with a background in Psychology), I wish to help you find confidence through life's inevitable and unforeseen changes, while balancing contentment versus extremism. There may not be a shiny toy or lifestyle at the end, but to live with contentment, and in all things, finding ways to respond and cope with change and hardships, that is the goal I am after.

My desire to help others was very real, however my issue was not dealing with my own erratic behavior and that led me down a path that could cause others harm if I didn't deal with it.

I was so enthusiastic about helping others, that at one point, I actually joined an online "Twilight Movie Saga Fan Club!" Maybe I joined this group to save people from the vampire obsession? Who knows.

Finally I started learning about evangelism and ministry through youth groups. I made it my intention to minister "understanding" to members of this online fan club. In my bio, I wrote a short piece sharing that I loved Twilight! One girl reached out to me, and we began talking. Her profile photo was scary. I saw sadness beyond her Marilyn Manson t-shirts, posters, choker-type necklaces, heavy eyeliner, and black hair that matched her black painted fingernails. I saw someone sad, lost and lonely.

That night I scheduled a time to talk with my Aunt about getting a ride for our trip to Duluth, Minnesota. I was also taking final exams in school before our summer break. Rather than focusing on what I needed to be doing, I was focusing on how to support *Zombie Jamie*. She was starting to open up to me rather quickly about her own abuse, and the hatred she felt toward others.

Mom had a strict rule that I had to be off the computer at a certain time, so I exchanged numbers with Jamie in order to talk with her more in-depth.

This is a great example of the Superhero Complex!

I spent an entire night talking with her about how I had found peace in my chaos. She was encouraged and inspired. I was telling her goodnight and she asked when we could speak again. I shared my schedule with her and told her we could speak the next evening. I told her I wouldn't be available to talk during the day while taking my final exams.

Fed Up

WHAT TO DO FOR SELF AND PEOPLE, JUSTICE SEEKER

When shunned from a church, I was angry. I felt protective of people who were still there under such leadership. I was protective of people who might be as mezmorized by the Pastor's allure as I was. I did not want anyone hurting like I'd been.

After being shunned, I crawled into myself for a while. Reverting to eating disorders and experiencing flaring suicidal ideation. When I'd find it in me to be energetically pissed off again, I would complain to firends and family about this community. Now, I've always encouraged people to avoid complaining about something unless they can change it soon after raising complaint. Was it up to me to change this community and protect people from it? No.

Name your concern. How will you impact it? If you can't then what? Heal yourself from it. In this church situation, it would have been wrong of me to try to destroy its reputation by spreading my gossip and distaste for their ways. I did not have a better place for them to go. I did not have unlimited resources or any energy to support their healing processes. I needed to trust God with them more than trusting myself with them. Once I approached this reality, I recognized the pain couldn't support restoration for anyone but at least for myself.

A friend of mine quit her job. The mission and vision of this workplace did not carry through with their promises for their staff. This hurt her heart very much. We talked in the beginning of her heart break. She'd wanted to warn others of the reality of this business. However, she agreed that it isn't her responsibility. Others will find out or learn themselves. We must quit playing God and trust people to God.

Jamie texted me the following morning. She was upset that we couldn't talk when she needed me most. I didn't quite know what to tell her. I apologized and encouraged her to find a way to keep calm and find peace. She was not listening to me. I decided to leave my phone in my locker during my first final exam, only to return to a phone receiving endless missed calls, voice mail messages and texts. Jamie was going mad.

She texted me things like, *"I've beaten up football players and eaten puppies. I will come to hurt you. If you don't respond to me, I will post photos of you on the internet saying, "I was touched by my Daddy and I liked it."* She wouldn't stop.

Her boyfriend worked at a prominent phone company, and apparently tapped into my phone contacts. They called and texted my most recent contacts spreading similar threats. I was shocked! I did not see this coming.

With friends, I went to deal with this the only way I knew how, by going to the school's counselor. I shared the texts and voicemails with her, unexpectedly, she said that no one would believe me. She said in her dealings with people like Jaime, she would only turn everything on me. I wasn't afraid, I was only annoyed.

I thought, "I know what to do. I've done this before. I will keep the evidence and know when to share it." I had her voice messages and text messages. When the policeman contacted her, he didn't have this information. He turned on me before I shared all the evidence. I filed a restraining order. I never did plan my summer trip to my Aunt's that year, simply because I was so distracted.

When was this going to stop? Did I have "Recycle the Victim" stamped on my forehead? Was I that naive? At times, it felt like I couldn't help but to be the bait to something innocent, with my good intentions skewed as something awful, grotesque, and abusive. Why?

This leads me to another story where I played Superhero but led me to victimization.

Big Sister, Little Sister was once a beautiful thing. The main focus in this was the friendship developed with your Little and the impact you have on their life. It existed to serve youth 6-18 years old. That was the organization and I'm sure it will continue to flourish well within its intended nature! However, the wholesome traditions did not carry on at my high school. Now, this program allowed a hazing tradition, as a form of passage or popularity initiation.

Rumors spread regarding this tradition, but I didn't fully understand it. In the cafeteria over lunch break, I asked my friends about it. They didn't have very good things to say about the history of Big Sister/Little Sister. They simply told me it was bad, and that I would hate being a part of the event. They told me I'd find it distasteful, offensive, and immature. I was far too curious to stop. It was my innate nature to think creatively, and have a curious mind. I was dramatic, and the thought of anything with fantasy related adventure intrigued me, so to stop me at this point, was like telling a cow not to eat grass. I had to know more.

You couldn't just show up and become a part of "Big Sister/Little Sister", but rather had to be invited to join their organization. If you were invited as a little sister, everyone considered you to be popular, and I had been invited.

One night, while on a shift at the local "Maurices Clothing Store", a big sister invited me. She told me I'd be out on a Sunday night with all the other Big and Little Sisters. She told me who would be my Big Sister. It would be a night of painting our nails, bonfires and sing-along songs! When they called, I only needed to confirm by telling my Mom I wanted to go, and she would let me.

I carried on with my plan to join, never considering popularity, but rather the chance of discovering what was behind this group, no matter how grotesque or unreputable I might find it to be.

I shared this with my friends the following day at lunch. My high school boyfriend at the time, didn't think much about it, but honestly, he didn't seem to think much of me either.

My investigation officially began. I'd been encouraged against it by friends, which only made me feel the need to dive deeper.

My best friend's grandmother passed away. Her funeral was to be Monday morning, the day after the wild night of initiation planned for us by the Big Sisters/Little Sisters. Knowing the situation and that I would be out all night, I was now forced with the decision to either go through with the initiation process, or attend my best friend's grandmother's funeral. I was feeling forced to choose and it was a very hard decision. I hated not being there for my friend, but something inside told me this initiation process was so very important to see all the way through.

I decided to go to the Principal's office to gain more clarity and understanding. What was this new tradition? Why was everyone so quiet and suspicious about it? He shared more with me about details of prior nights and how local policemen and the school tried to shut this down. The girls knew just what to do, and what they needed in order to keep their initiation a secret, as well as protect it during the hazings.

I asked why the school and policemen couldn't shut it down. He told me it would take someone on the inside to turn it in, so they had enough evidence and information.

I went home and shared this new information with my Mom. I told her about my opportunity to take charge, and shut this hazing tradition down. Neither of us really understood the depths of these people's actions quite yet.

The phone rang and the girls asked my Mom's permission to pick me up from our house. Mom turned to look at me awaiting my confirmation. I shook my head yes, and then apologized to my best friend for not being there for her. I knew she'd have family and more friends to support her. I just *had* to shut this down the only way I knew how.

I heard their car with its music blasting and the horn

honking in the driveway. I was told to come with pajamas and a change of clothes. These Big Sisters lost all class as soon as they arrived at our home. They began yelling at me to get in the car.

As soon as I was in the car, I was greeted with crass language and a book of songs to memorize. This book also told us where we'd be, plus all the rules. I didn't have a chance to respond as they blasted their music and took us on to our first destination. I cannot remember all of the lyrics to the songs we were singing. I've asked other Little Sisters to share the lyrics with me and they wouldn't even respond. Is there still a fear of the *Big Sisters*?

I feel the girls *still* wish to dissociate from me concerning this topic. This event was something that continued annually out of pride, anger, boredom and the need to fulfill revenge. What I did not understand was, how following suit with insanity would bring a sense of fulfillment. If you were hurt the prior year, how would hurting someone else in a harsher manner bring closure? For some unknown reason, this vengeance created a very important ripple effect. It was almost a *purge* of emotions or an opportunity to finally let out societal frustration from person to person, year to year, lifting the weighty burden from yourself.

At our first stop, we met the Big Sisters. We practiced our song. This is all I remember of the lyrics: "*We are the sister girls, we wear our hair in curls....*" The rest was vulgar, it was embarrassing, so I think my mind must have chosen to block it out. We called ourselves *bitches and sluts*.

At the first stop, we were told to wear certain clothes. Once changed into the outfits approved by them, we stood in a line where Big Sisters threw a variety of foods and condiments on us. A few sisters had dog treats and we were ordered to eat these treats as a reward for our behavior and obedience. We were also told to eat spicy, pickled condiments. I knew better than to do this; because I was a walking food pyramid, I could just spit out the gross food onto my shoulder. These girls were so focused on their pride they would never notice where I spit out. I was covered with food anyway, so it blended right in.

I made my decision and stood firm. That's exactly what I would do to escape putting horrible, inedible foods into my digestive system.

Our next stop was the beach. All big sisters brought their little sisters for another round of shenanigans by the lake in town.

We were already tired, scared, and wishing this whole ordeal would come to an end. On our drive to the lake, we were each given dog treats for our good behavior. The big sisters told us they'd check to make sure we ate them, and there would be consequences if we did not. They drove us in an old bronco, with a rusted trunk. It was so rusted in places that there were holes in the flooring.

Instead of eating my dog treat, I put it through the hole in the trunk and watched it skip across the highway. I encouraged the rest of the girls to do it too, but they were so encompassed with fear that they wouldn't. They actually believed the big sisters would go back, find them and figure out who didn't eat them.

Now that we were running and singing our demeaning "Sister Girls" song, skipping all the way, dressed in condiments, and God knows what else, we were losing stamina.

We were told to run to the red phone booth, which was less than a mile from the lake. The big sisters met us at the red phone booth and told us what we needed was for every little sister to fit into that small, red phone booth.

So many smudges were on that phone booth, you could say, we definitely left our mark. Even much later, you could see the residue of stains and smudges left from that night. It's no wonder the city removed it, for now if you look, that red phone booth is no longer there.

Once we returned to the beach, others joined. Guys and gals from high school who'd already been deemed the popular ones were there too. They came to carry on the hazing. As they showed up, Big Sisters were notified that cops were coming to check on the scene. This gave them plenty of time to avoid showing what was coming next for us.

I consider this the most demeaning act of the night. They had us sing our anthem then run into the water. I began to wonder why some of the big sisters gained a sympathetic eye when they looked over at me.

The water felt quite refreshing since running and sweating with all of those condiments covering us from head to toe.

Some guys showed up with hot dogs that served as their prop. One by one I saw guys grab a little sister and lead them to their knees, commanding them to perform a blow job on the hot dog balancing in the guy's open zipper of their jeans. This was awful. This was a trigger for me and the big sisters got wind of it.

Pretty soon, many were recalling that I was the girl who spoke about turning her father in for sexual abuse at *that event* in town.

Some of these girls had been at the event, and knew this would be hard for me. They knew that I could potentially turn them in for these inappropriate acts. If they were beginning to get soft on anyone, I felt it was me.

They kept their eyes on me, maybe to protect me, assuring themselves I was all right, but probably more-so to make sure I would not turn them in. Well, all of their seemingly good intentions were about to go down the drain and very quickly. They were way too late for this girl. I would be the one to turn them in!

Throughout the night, my anger increased. Big Sisters from the year prior, even girls in their freshman and sophomore year of college, drove all the way home on this night just for Big Sister/ Little Sister. They came to the beach already drunk out of their mind, and ready to make trouble.

They began yelling and throwing things like glass jars and bottles, demanding that big sisters put more fear into us, because *they* certainly would if they were in charge. They said they were not being hard enough on them.

The sunlight was replaced by moonlight as these wild

girls yelled, louder and louder, demanding tougher acts to be performed on the little sisters. The big sisters tried to keep them from making a scene large enough to potentially involve the police. It was so out of control that the "Bigs" in charge of us had a yelling match with the drunk, out of control, former bigs.

I wound up wandering by myself. I walked to the other side of the Pavilion building on the lake, beside a playground, when out of the corner of my eye, I caught a girl running after me. She was tripping and stumbling on her way to me. At first, I was afraid and ran a few steps from her. I then ran to the steps leading to the slide on the top of the playground.

I recognized how slow and klutzy this girl was. She was drunk, with a large jar of spicy peppers, which she intended to force me to eat. Noticing her physical and mental state, I stood before the slide and crossed my arms as she attempted to crawl up the slide towards me. She told me, "Eat this you bitch!" I said, "No. I don't like spicy things." She probably didn't even hear me. I wasn't afraid of her. When she reached closer to me with the jar, I grabbed her wrist and flung it away, so that the jar fell from her hands and shattered on the sidewalk. She was *so tough* at this point, she started running away from me, calling me crazy.

The night continued with these insane Moments. Next, we went to a large bonfire party. As we arrived, having avoided eating our dog treats altogether, we stepped out of the bronco, into a swarm of the most attractive and popular kids in our school.

Even my friends who advised me not to go to this, were there joining the hazing activities. Now, we were made to swim in a kiddie pool. Rumors had it, the kiddie pool was filled with cow intestines. It might have been true, because it did smell and feel as though it could have been. I was tired and ready for this night to end, I suppose this made me a bit feisty, so I yelled "Mosh pit!" and we ran faster in the pool, laughing and stumbling about. A Big yelled at me for attempting to make the Littles smile.

Then we had to sing our song again, while running laps

around the bonfire, as the surrounding people spit at us and disgustingly cursed.

These were people purposely staying up late, premeditating their *opportunity* to spit and curse at younger girls. I needed a break.

I stepped away in the dark woods, and began writing down the names of as many people as I could remember seeing there. I also wrote down the places I'd been, as well as the things they made us do. I didn't want to leave out any details. I had this, and I would expose them.

We were then shuffled into multiple cars and brought to one of the big sister's houses. There we stood beside the horse fence, as they hosed us off with cold water. We needed to do *this* before we could set foot in their homes, taking a maximum of another 3 minute shower before "going to sleep."

I was panicking; I had to work at a retail shop the next day and I smelled awful. It was impossible to have everything removed in a freezing cold, 3 minute shower. Of course, the big sisters got their shower first, having hot water and longer showers.

I remember leaving the bathroom and joining the living room with all the big and little sisters. The groups split up, sleeping at two seperate places; the big's parent's house.

Here, the big sisters talked with us about the plans for the following day. They told us that we were not allowed to fall asleep until the last big sister fell asleep. We lay there, watching and waiting, until all of the Big sisters were finally asleep.

Still I wonder, why we as people allow others to have such control over our lives. Is it a standing fear of not being accepted? If we do not bow to the tactics and practices of others, the result can be bullying or even worse. Many are sometimes bullied by these types of people for no reason at all. Bullying is a terrible, cruel thing, and needs advocates to bring it to an end.

Many young people even now, perhaps far worse than I experienced, succumb as victims to these bullying tactics. They do not know how to free themselves from them . We must stand against this form of abuse. Bullying, hazing, and other cruelties used to wreak havoc on the innocent, whether emotionally, mentally, or physically must come to an end. This will always be wrong.

That awful night finally came to a close. We awoke very early the next morning to dress for breakfast, before going back to the high school. Everyone was kind at breakfast. It seemed that the same sympathy as before, arose in the big sisters when they saw me. I was quiet and they hadn't a clue of the crumpled piece of paper I was keeping. I wrote every person's name, where we went and all I'd seen the night before. It's just what the Principle said he needed to shut this down.

I walked quietly on my way to History Class with Mr. Elliot. I looked up to him, as many did. He was kind, considerate, funny and a great teacher. He was also the wrestling coach. I typically sat in the front row of class, but on this day I saw the shame in his eyes pouring over me as I showed up to class a bit late, making my way to another seat.

I felt that he expected more from me because I took part in this event. I couldn't bear to sit in the class that entire time knowing how disappointed he was in me. I left class quickly before the bell dismissed us. I walked toward the Principal's office to fulfill my mission to end this hazing tradition!

Of course, there were a few people I ran into along the way. Some of the big sisters saw me walking in the hall and asked if I was all right. I nodded, "yes" and they told me they were here for me if I needed anything.

I walked away from them as they said that. I saw my boyfriend in the commons area. He was a real dud; lazy, and unsupportive regarding anything I needed. Still, I told him what I was about to do, and he called me stupid for it.

I had crushes on boys before, but after abuse, I hadn't actually settled down with anyone for a while. My first boyfriend, after sexual abuse, was a short fling. I then found someone new the following summer. My best friend and I went on a double date and at the end of it, swapped mates! I connected with Aiden much more than the other guy. We sang, spent quality time with our mutual friends, and performed in "Battle of the Bands" together. Aiden was fun, lively and free spirited. I had so much fun with him! However, he did not back me up on important things, such as when I felt I needed to shut this hazing tradition down. He talked down to me. He was my prom date and the dance was coming up soon, but I couldn't have his lack of support at this time. So we entered into our first spat, and I walked away from him.

I continued making my way to the principal's office, I somehow managed to get through without knocking. Sitting down at his desk, setting the crumpled piece of paper before him, I told him he now had everything he needed in order to shut this operation down.

I then walked to my locker, called my Mom to come and pick me up from school so that I could sleep at home. I quit my job over the phone on the walk to meet my Mom, and I wept in the car. That was an awful night and on the 49th anniversary of it happening. I knew it probably would not be a happy ending, especially for me, not quite yet.

Prom was coming up and I was the Post Prom Committee President. It was up to me to handle all details of prom with our team. One choice I faced was whether or not to allow these girls to attend their senior prom. I made my choice by turning them in, but I became one uncomfortable girl. These girls were close to one another, looking forward to their senior prom.

I was the odd duck out, still, I wanted to be fair. They didn't deserve it, but that's not why I allowed them to go to prom. I wanted to be the bigger person, and I wanted them to recognize it. That was my wishful thinking because most of these girls were so self-absorbed and couldn't possibly see they were in the wrong.

They all followed suit with one another the night of prom.

My boyfriend bought his prom ticket late. Being mine was free, we could have been in the front of the line for our coronation walk. Because of his last minute purchase, he and I were the very last couple to walk. This meant I was at the end of the line, slowly approaching the catwalk. I endured each glare from every person before me. People whispering and calling me names, some even barking at me, insinuating I was a bitch.

I had so many feelings going on in my head, but I felt so awkward, awful, and out of place. Adults were telling me I made a good choice, while my peers only objective was to make me regret this. I was a teenager, and the most important thing to a teenager is to feel confidence, and a sense of belonging. This should not have been my weight to carry, but it is how the awful tradition ended, and therefore it's a part of my story forever.

My date was not the least bit chivalrous, nor proud to be my date. Gratefully, my sweet friend Lyndsey was there! Her date was being lame as well, and so she and I danced the night away! We decided not to worry about anyone else, and enjoyed the rest of our night.

After I'd danced my fears away, I began to ignore the people who were against me, and never for me. At this point of my mostly, unpleasant, halfway turned nice evening, the Varsity Girls Basketball Captain walked up to me.

If there ever was a living Barbie doll, this girl fit the image. She was confident, kind and smart, with her blonde hair, tan skin, and athletic body gracefully gliding across the floor in a Pink gown, very befitting of Cinderella. She walked up to me, tapping me on my shoulder. As I turned towards her, she unexpectedly hugged and thanked me.

This shocked me, as well as others, I'm sure. In front of everyone who now despised me, she thanked me for shutting this down with such bravery. She single handedly changed how people looked at me from that point on. She graduated that year and I haven't seen her since that dance, but she holds a special place in my heart as the angel at prom, when no one else would be as kind to me.

Even though the angel at prom helped me get through that night, the remainder of that school year was awful for me. Girls and boys continued to bark at me. They would also bark and bully anyone else who associated with me. Because of this, teachers became hall monitors before class to shut down any hazing behavior. People I thought were my friends stepped away from me. I felt disowned and shunned by everyone there, except the teachers.

In high school it's natural to want to be accepted by our peers. We are not as aware of older people's opinions about us as much as our friend's opinions and people our own age. We want so much to fit in and be accepted by friends. Bullying should never be an acceptable behavior, and because it was tolerated in this school, I felt extremely frustrated.

I did receive plenty of gratitude in the form of letters of appreciation and flowers from some of the Moms of children at our school. That was what I now refer to as "a kind band aid".

Would I choose now the same decisions I made then, now that I've tasted the consequences? Absolutely. I would turn everyone in all over again. I would break the Big Sister, Little Sister traditions they held so sacred and dear, so that no one would ever be hurt by them again. It was absurd, ridiculous and very immature to think anyone would commit to hazing, thinking it was a good idea.

Many big sisters lost their college scholarships because of their actions in this event. Others served consequences by their parents, which seems mild in comparison.

I had trouble believing people could do this to others, believing it was perfectly okay and acceptable, just because of tradition which had remained in this place for many prior years. Would you hurt someone else simply because it was done to you first? As an adult, does that make sense? These girls were all nearly adults, so were the guys. I wonder if they realized that there might be consequences for their actions. Why do some people bully people and never get caught?

" IT'S BIGGER THAN OPTIMISM, AND
MORE POWERFUL THAN FREEDOM.
FORGIVENESS IS MANY THINGS,
HELPING SHED THE WEIGHT OF
A BURDEN CONCOCTED BY PAIN
AND ELECTRIFIED BY TRIGGERS.
FORGIVENESS RESTARTS EVERYTHING;
ALL IS NEW AND THE CONTROL OVER
YOUR LIFE IS RESTORED BACK TO YOU
AND NOT WITH YOUR OFFENDER. "

Third Chapter

In 2020 I spent intentional time desensitizing and reprocessing my harsh memories through a therapy called EMDR (Eye Movement Desensitization and Reprocessing Therapy). In some of these sessions, my friend and Doctor, Phil, would perform a technique called "brainspotting" with me. This body-brain psychotherapy technique suggests that where you look affects how you feel. BSP is a new type of therapy that has truly helped me to access, process, and overcome trauma and negative emotions.

Dr. Phil B. performed this technique with me in February of 2020 when I learned of my ten year highschool reunion approaching. I did not want to return home with similar feelings of being an outsider, frustrated by the immaturity of my peers, or those in the class above me. Through BSP, I can confidently say that this issue has been resolved and I believe I will quite enjoy my class reunion. I walk in truth that what I did was good, helpful and brave. I can move on from this now, while enjoying people where they are in their journey.

These familiar situations did not stop. I was working at a Boys and Girls Club Thrift Store after school hours the following year. It was a very good time in my life. I loved my job, the staff, and working at this store. Sometimes, people were assigned to this store to work their community hours. We called these people the jailbirds.

This was good for them, but not so great for me. For some reason, their very presence made me feel once again recyclable, like that tiny abused little girl. It happened twice that I had the same problem with two different men.

The first incident happened after man #1 clocked out, and came to my register to check out his purchases. He was one of those guys who would walk around anywhere, with music blasting through his cell phone speaker from the pocket of his low riding pants. I could see his pregnant girlfriend down the aisle. I guess he thought she would not hear him playing "Birthday Sex" on his phone while checking out. He then handed me his cell phone number on a slip of paper, while looking me in the eye, lip-syncing the song to me.

I was able to move on from this, but man #2 was far worse. Maybe he didn't realize how he came off. He certainly thought he was charming, but to me he was unrelenting and irritating. He wore outdated shirts with dragons on them, baggy jeans, an eyebrow piercing and a low ponytail. When I first met him, he was a kind guy, but as time progressed he became the irritating man I just described.

This irritating man began talking with me during shifts. While his chattering didn't bother me, he soon became harassing and annoying.

He started by winking, and smiling at me often. Did this man think his actions were acceptable behavior? I felt so confused as to why this man chose me to be the object of his affection, with my anorexic body frame, nose and eyebrow piercing, right down to my cute little pixie cut hair. There was definitely a large age gap difference, but absolutely nothing stopped him.

I started pretending to be on the phone every time this man was around. One day, after I clocked out of work, I drove to the gas station and noticed he was following me. I felt uncomfortable yet thought, could this be a coincidence that we are getting gas at the same time? He started filling his gas tank then walked toward me and started a conversation. I began to feel uncomfortable. He had a long pause and just stared at me. As he stared at me, I dialed my boyfriend's number and was very glad he answered. Pretending the call was an incoming call, I answered, "Hello?"

My boyfriend seemed confused as I started making small talk. I made him so confused, telling him I was on my way to see him, hoping this man would hear what I was saying and just leave. Staying on the phone, I left my car and entered the gas station.

As I returned to my car, this man's vehicle was no longer in the same place. He had moved it and suddenly appeared from his parked car. I was no longer on my phone call, now feeling trapped and awkward.

I cringed, now knowing he was still there waiting for me. He approached me slowly, beginning to tell me the strangest things. "We can't tell my wife. She's the jealous type." I didn't know what to say to him. I only knew I needed to get out of there fast, so I lifted my phone up again, pretending to answer another phone call and quickly left.

It was the most awkward and confusing Moment ever. That irritating man must have found my phone number in the back office of our workplace. That same night, he sent many text messages, telling me he couldn't wait to be with me, encouraging me to avoid his wife, that she was the jealous type who wouldn't approve of our relationship." This man and I never talked about this gas station encounter again.

There's something else about that situation that happened to me though. It left me feeling dirty, as though I had done something wrong. I felt gross, confused, and more than anything, violated, not knowing how to handle it. Maybe it was because he wasn't the first creep, but now I was seeing the truth that there are many men with inappropriate behavior and it doesn't mean I did anything wrong, but I do need to keep my guard up at all times.

Of course, I was smart enough to know that his wife, the woman who vowed her life in marriage to him, wouldn't appreciate his fantasy of an affair with a minor! This was more than a teenager should ever have to deal with, still I kept thinking if I had done anything to provoke this. What had I done to deserve these advances of older men over and over? Why was I repetitively the object of a perverted man's attention and unduly placed affection?

This man was also a friend to the assistant manager. She knew this irritating man and got him the job. I had to go about this correctly. I needed them to believe me. Fortunately, by now I learned to save all paper trails. First, I needed to let the assistant manager know, while respecting the woman involved, as I let her know of my major concerns about my safety with this man. There was just one problem; she didn't believe me. After I told her, she talked with him and unfortunately, she bought into his lies and deception. This left me no hope that I would ever convince her he did such a thing. I did not share my paper trail with *her* as to avoid making more friction with her, and decided to wait to show my boss.

He was her friend. It was brushed under the rug until I went to the big boss and showed him the texts from this man, then I said, "He leaves or I do." Things were taken care of, he was asked to leave, no longer allowed near me ever again. I know this irritating man stepped in my boss's office with the assistant manager to look over the texts together. I do not know what else happened in that room, but I knew that my boss had my back.

It took me a long time to forgive this man, not only because he was a perverted older man stalking me, but also because he was someone who made me feel uncomfortable, and triggered the "victim mentality" I felt before and it was something I thought I had dealt with. That is something many people deal with, and it's hard.

After that incident with him, I became overtly fearful that older men would stalk me for the rest of my life. I had to forgive his inappropriate behavior, while keeping my boundaries set around men. I felt I had to forgive him in order to let go of the fear of *predator recycling*.

I believe many women experience this after they've been stalked or abused once before. There is a familiarity about the men, like the woman's first offender, that follows her until she combats it with forgiveness and boundaries. Even after receiving therapy, after setting boundaries and after forgiving, remember your weak spot and always remember and acknowledge your achilles heel.

Many in my life thought it unnecessary to forgive him, but I was learning about the power of forgiveness. You see, forgiving him was really for me, more than it ever was about him. Forgiving him changed my mindset and heart posture. This shift was far more important to me than the actual act of forgiveness. I was also moved by the effect it would have on him. It was a personal thing that I knew I needed to do. I knew if I forgave him, another chain would break.

One part of forgiveness is a gift for yourself. It brings you closure, rest and release from offenses you fell victim to. Then comes compassion and empathy for your offender.

The second part of forgiveness is the powerful and beautiful gift it can give our offenders. This works when the offender is able to receive our forgiveness. If received, our offender will experience this *invitation* to a second chance. We must consider our boundaries and what this second chance looks like. One cannot forgive without setting boundaries. If setting boundaries without forgiveness, those boundaries will quickly become walls that hinder us from the compassion and empathy we could be gifted in this process.

When I saw the irritating man, several years later, that is

when I knew I needed to forgive him. There was a town parade and street fair. I was modeling in the window of a clothing store; they called my friend and I "live window mannequins", and this man walked by.

I could see the increasing discomfort in his eyes, as he saw me for the first time in many years. At first, he was trying to see if I was real or an actual mannequin, then he recognized me and looked like he had frozen over. He gripped his wife's hand tightly, seemingly to assure her that he had chosen her, he was hers, and no one else's.

This let me know just how much guilt he felt about the prior situation. Whatever his intention at the parade, I finally knew in my heart that I truly had no longer carried ill thoughts toward this man.

In that Moment, he became just like any other person walking around the street fair.

Now would I trust him? Well, that would be another matter entirely. I learned that forgiveness and trust really are two very separate issues. One can forgive, but need not trust the person in order to do so. I am so glad I've learned the difference.

Older men were stalking me, hitting on me, without my consent. Every one of their flirtatious moves disgusted me.

I had no idea more situations like this would arise, but they certainly did. It was okay that I waited to forgive him. I would face many more of these situations causing me fear and disgust for those involved, and it really wasn't until 2020 that I was able to fully release, forgive and let go of experiences like this.

I thought the stalking was over, but I have more stories. Remember when my Mom moved into a new, larger house in a beautiful neighborhood called Sunset Hills? I enjoyed my neighbors and neighborhood. One summer, we were all excited as we expected new neighbors soon. All we knew about this couple was that they were moving from California. We all felt eager and curious to meet them.

On the day this family moved into our development, my cousin and I decided to take a walk from our house down to the beach. It was a hot summer day in Minnesota; one of those days I've experienced many times, where the heat exhausts you, taking your breath away, leaving you parched, dry and unmotivated to do anything. Walking back home became a chore for us at this point.

Suddenly, a red convertible pulled up beside us. When asked where we were headed, the man said he recognized me as his new neighbor. This older gentleman offered us a ride home, and though it seemed harmless at the time, we both felt it unwise, so we expressed our gratitude and turned down his offer, we kept walking.

School began, and with this new season, our new neighbors brought their two grandchildren to live with them. They quickly asked if we could babysit and help their grandchildren get on and off the school bus. I was eager to help, so we made an agreement. On the nights I'd babysit, I could use their in-home tanning bed, once the kids were asleep. My pay was $10 an hour whether they were awake or asleep, and the tanning bed was free.

As a teenage girl, I thought this must have been the best agreement I'd ever made. I had plans to attend the "Sadie Hawkins Dance", and with this new tan, I was now more excited about this plan!

Nearer to the school dance, Mom decided she would host our new neighbors for a bonfire and drinks, adults only. Later that following day, she told me the old Californian man came over and made a strange comment to her... "*I came home today, and opened the garage door. I saw your daughter's feet in the tanning bed and was like WOAH, gotta get outta here!"* He laughed nervously and no one knew how to respond to that. His story was so out of the blue, so he appeared socially awkward and nervous.

When Mom told me this, I remembered him giving me a tour of his home the first night of my babysitting job. I remember feeling slightly freaked out, but wasn't positive I needed to be concerned.

He showed me to the tanning room (in the garage), taught me how to use the tanning bed, and where the cleaning supplies were for cleaning the bed after each use. Before leaving the garage, he pointed to a black box in the back left corner of the room. He told me not to worry about that box with the blinking red light. He told me it was the garage door opener and not a camera...I did feel strange for a Moment. That feeling was quickly replaced by my teenage excitement about this dance with a boy and my tan skin.

About a month later, his granddaughter ran to our house late at night, pounding on the front door. Upon opening the door, she ran into my room, then began crying under my covers. She told me her Grandpa touched her inappropriately, and it scared her. She then told me she saw me on their homemade videos. I was shocked! This poor girl, and how could they film me?

The next morning, I stuck a post-it note to their front door, saying their granddaughter had been with me overnight, requesting she stay the night again. I told them I'd make sure she'd get to school and back.

Already contemplating the right thing to do, I went to the school at day's end to pick her up. I couldn't find her anywhere. I looked for her to get on the bus, but never saw her. Once we got home, there was a huge "For Sale" sign in their yard. I assumed they packed immediately, leaving with their grandchildren. There was no way I could help these kids now.

After telling my Mom what was going on, she wanted us to drop it. Mom didn't want us going to court again, so here I was, with nothing but a burning hole of justice in my heart.

All I could do was hope and pray she would trust someone enough to reach out again with the truth. I've never forgotten her. I will always wonder how her life turned out. Did her innocence become devoured by her sick grandfather? Or was his being caught this time enough to set him on a better path, one that would see her as the sweet and innocent 6-year-old girl she was?

Third Chapter

I wrote this book with purpose. That purpose is set to support people where they are, while promoting mental health awareness and healing. Many of my social media followers, friends and family members have shared the impact this has already had in their life. Sharing our story can carry so much power and invite others to heal, unlocking the truth that they are not alone.

A couple men on my book's Facebook group were impacted and shared how they were affected by my transparency. I felt so excited to be helping people through the book, even before it was set to publish!

At this time, I was seeking the possibility of an agent. Maybe I would have someone do the work to market my speaking engagements. If you don't want to or can't do it, hire someone else!

After several conversations with a man about the agent position, I decided to meet with him. I went to collect information about him at my favorite local pizzeria, "Providence Pizza". This was a safe place for me to meet strangers, because I wasn't a stranger to the staff there. I wrote most of this book while there, eating pizza!

This man talked the talk, but I wasn't sure he was capable of doing more. He shared his resume and upon doing so, asked more questions about my story and my life than I thought appropriate. He asked me about my desires for the book. It was about this time I started noticing a switch in his gaze and his intentions towards me. Upon noticing him becoming flirtatious, I switched gears getting ready to leave for the night. I thanked him for his time, and for not having any ulterior motives. I told him that I was very grateful he didn't! I then explained what I meant by ulterior motives and how other men have had them towards me. I went on to explain ulterior motives because I knew he had them, and I wanted to make everything clear. I could see his wheels spinning.

Not too much later, after leaving our meeting, I received an email from this man. He told me how much he appreciated me, and felt it would be okay for us to date. He explained that he did not have any ulterior motives, but that as he spoke with me, he became interested in me and hoped I'd consider a romantic relationship with him.

Upon my rejection of his proposal, he became upset and defensive. I had caught him. He was a guy with more than a silly crush, but with ulterior motives concerning my business. It felt slimy; I felt he wanted to own how I moved, where and with whom. I said no and laid down a thick boundary line. This took a shot at his pride. We have not talked since. If I think about it, it is funny he met with me to promote this book. Well, he made his way into the book!

This next situation is still difficult for me to talk about. After this experience, I locked myself in my apartment, too paralyzed to leave, and fearful this person would be around the next corner.

He sent me a private online message, sharing how my transparency had been helpful and refreshing for him. I thanked him and congratulated him on his healing process. He carried on the conversation, seeking a way to support me. I told him I was grateful for his encouragement and the support I already had.

It became a painful conversation that I couldn't seem to end. This guy couldn't seem to make a point in his conversation. Finally, he messaged me that he really wanted to help me financially. He hoped to meet me in person to share why he'd give money, and how much he'd donate. This felt unreal and nerve racking.

As for accountability, I contacted my financial planner to seek her advice concerning how to accept donations. Being we hadn't had anything official up to this point, we decided he could simply contact her concerning any financial donations toward the book. I then connected the two of them, so they could discuss tax write-off details. For some reason, he did not want to talk to her alone.

Regardless of how often I reminded him to talk with her, he simply wouldn't. He emailed *me,* telling me how he wanted to give. He even offered me his laptop! He seemed a very generous person!

First, he asked to meet with me, so I gave him 40 minutes at a nearby Barnes and Noble. We met in the Starbucks Cafe, where I had my Psychology classmate meeting me for our class project. I texted her that I didn't know the man I'd be meeting, so if I needed a scapegoat, she would need to rescue me creatively. I told her I'd text her the word, "Help".

By this time, after my experiences, I at least learned not to be with a man I didn't know and couldn't trust, alone.

During our meeting, this man opened up to me, sharing

hardships that have really affected his life. I applauded his transparency and thanked him for telling me that *my* book supported his decision to begin seeking professional support!

He proceeded to tell me he wished to thank me. He gave me a necklace, then told me he wanted to give me a very large sum of money. I was in disbelief. This was too good to be true. He couldn't be doing this out of the kindness of his heart alone, yet, I have known people to do so. Was there a catch? I couldn't tell yet.

My financial planner and I weren't too sure if we could believe him, so we tried to keep cool, calm and collected. We set our minds to be okay with or without the donation.

If he gave the money, then amazing! The book would have been paid for right then, and I would continue writing without needing to work! I was excited and trying not to have my hopes too high.

He contacted me often, more often than I expected or wished. I continued to redirect him to my financial planner, to discuss anything of financial matters. He was going back and forth on if he should give me the money or not. I wasn't sure why at the beginning, but I told him he was not obligated. Whether he wanted to or not, he needed to decide so I could plan and move forward.

He then set up to bring me a new laptop. I was beginning to feel very uncomfortable with his comments and how often he contacted me, rather than my financial planner, but I did need a new laptop.

I had my classmate meet him in the parking lot to collect the laptop. I thanked him in a text message and carried on. I didn't walk to campus alone anymore. I was beginning to fear him as he would often call me in panic mode, hyperventilating about whether or not he should do *this* or *that*. I didn't understand why, so calmly, I asked him, "Why is this a hard decision for you to make?" He told me he asked his Mom to pray for *us*, because he truly felt I was to become his wife. He admitted he did not know how to pursue me, but felt this was it, we were meant to be together. He said he wasn't even sure I noticed his love for me. If this was unrequited, he wasn't sure he could donate the money, or if God was actually leading him to do this.

I responded by telling him I was not dating at the time. I told him I was waiting to date until after the book would be near the finish line. I also told him I had feelings for another guy, anyway. I was not attracted to this guy in the least bit and I was direct about it.

Again, I gave him an out. I told him he needed to discuss finances with my financial planner and not with me. I told him I wasn't expecting anything, and that he needed to make a decision. This book would publish with or without his generous donation and this back and forth was exhausting.

I truly thought *that* would be the end of my conversations with him. And, it was over, at least for a while, until the night my friend Nick came to my apartment to help me hang wallpaper. I was posting silly photos of Nick and me messing around as we applied the wallpaper. We were having fun! In response to my silly photos shared to my social media account, I received a message from this obsessive guy.

He was angry. He expressed to me how much he hated that I was with this guy at all. He suspiciously presumed we were dating. By this time, I was fed up with his infatuation with me. I told him that Nick was not my boyfriend, and even if he were, or anyone else for that matter, that I had the freedom to decide when and with whom I wanted to date. I let him know, once again, that my personal life was not any of his business. He was out of line. I told him he needed to stop contacting me. I felt I expressed this to him directly, and *in no uncertain terms*, but he did not understand this.

He continued to weigh in about his donations, contacting me through email messages, talking back and forth about whether or not he could keep up with this commitment. He would say that God told him to do so, then take it back because he fell in love with me. This happened over the course of one week of *knowing* me. Being his feelings were unrequited, he said his initial offer might feel too overwhelming. He told me how anxious he felt about this, but wanted to try to make it work. He told me he asked his Mom to pray for *us* and *our love*. I thought, "what love is he talking about? I don't know him!"

I never blamed this man. I know he had a troubled past and simply felt inspired by my stories and mission. His feelings changed and grew quickly because he saw *hope*. He misinterpreted this *hope* as a romantic feeling toward me, and became infatuated with this fantasy. What happened broke my heart, so I wished to show as much support as I could. Having experienced my end of a story like this in the past, I knew better than to carry my former Superhero Complex, I knew I could not be his savior platonically or romantically. I had to draw the line.

I finally told him I did not want his help in any way. He emailed me over and over again, wanting to apologize and reconnect.

I felt grossed out by the situation, and he certainly wasn't anyone I wanted in my life at that point. I blocked his phone number and blocked him from all social media accounts.

One Friday night I went to a worship service and he was there in that big, mega church. I saw him as I talked to the boy I did have a crush on. I saw him stare at me, while I was talking with this crush, we'll call him *John*. I cut the conversation short, as I saw John sit down. This guy went to sit straight behind him. I was so nervous, that I didn't care if John thought I was creepy and staring at him. I actually felt protective. I walked away to breathe in the bathroom and came out to see my stalker standing outside the bathrooms, waiting to say hello and ask how I was doing. I told him I was fine, then left.

I would carry on after talking with the church security, to assure that if he approached me again, they'd intervene. I felt safer to tell the staff at my hotspot pizzeria what was going on, so that if this guy would appear there, they'd help me. I was very encouraged to get people on my side, and loved ones were nervous for me as well.

He was quiet for a while. Having the church security approach him was enough to keep him away for a while. It wasn't too long though, before he emailed me again, that he wanted to see me, to talk and apologize. I told him that wouldn't be necessary. There was no reason for us to get together and talk. I was very direct with him.

He then said he couldn't handle this heartache, and so he was going to move away. Personally, I was relieved, until receiving yet *another* email from him, a couple months later. He was back, and wanted to visit as if nothing had happened. As if he wasn't scaring me enough, or trying to control the situation, I panicked and called my counselor for help.

This situation is still difficult for me to talk about. I locked myself in my apartment, too paralyzed to leave, fearful that he would be around the corner. My counselor drove me to the police department to file a restraining order, in case he did show up at my apartment. The family I nannied for, felt it best I stay home, just in case he followed me while with their kids. I didn't leave my apartment for two weeks. I didn't post on social media about where I was and I didn't talk with anyone, but my Grandma who was my roommate at the time. I didn't drive anywhere, because I feared he might find me and follow me. He didn't care about how he was scaring me, it didn't seem like he could grasp that he was scaring me at all.

Finally, the date came, when he said he would be returning to his new home out of state. He emailed me about it twice, *once* to see if we could have coffee before he left, but I ignored his email. The *second* email was to say he is sorry he had missed me, that he would try again next time.

I broke down and cried so hard, having to process leaving my apartment without fear that he'd still be in the Kansas City area looking for me. I never did see him again, after this, but everything he did left its mark on me for a while. I was overwhelmed by fear because of the things he said to me over emails.

For the first time in two weeks, I left my home. I went with my grandmother to breakfast, and actually drove my car. I was still slightly uncomfortable. This was a huge step for me because I still imagined he was nearby, knowing my address, or seeing my car. I cried at the relief I had in making that step, and felt so grateful to have family with me.

When you've dealt with trauma in the past, and something triggers you, reminding you of your former traumatic experiences, it can leave you crippled once again, taking weeks to recuperate. Regardless of how long ago the traumatic experience was, we must always offer grace to those suffering with PTSD. We haven't walked in their shoes, we haven't seen what they've seen or been where they've been.

Trauma can flicker in your mind's eye like lightening upon a thundering trigger and set you off course for a while. It takes patience, grace and empathy from our friends and family to get us back on track.

At this point, how could I ever trust I would one day have a normal relationship with a man, after all I'd been through? Did this man even have a clue about what he was doing to me emotionally, after trying to control my situation? He wanted to give me large amounts of money, give me jewelry, have me marry him and be happy with it, without my consent or even love, for that matter. How could I let go of my fear of men when the ones who decided they wanted me, dictated the details in such a short time? How could I even trust *good intentions* from men at this point?

The one man (Dad) who was to protect me, provide good examples, show me the standard I should attain to find love, had destroyed any clarity on what to expect. Men seemed to line up right behind him, to assure me, that I wouldn't have quality standards for the romantic relationship for the rest of my life. Something had to change.

I learned what to do, based on what not to do. I learned who to trust by seeking the opposite of those I learned I couldn't trust.

I was that little girl, living in her Dad's constant partying lifestyle, walking each day through the family basement, that could look like a nightclub for perverts, with hidden secrets and unseen back rooms, one you might see on an Adult X rated, unfiltered movie.

To flee from the self harm and addiction, from what this life had introduced me to, I turned to the extreme opposite, the church.

I wanted to find my self worth. I also wanted to broaden my focal point beyond the hardships I went through, and beyond the harm done against me. This meant, trying to erase the memories of my past, while opening my heart to the healing process ahead of me.

One way I did this was to begin surrounding myself with people who knew how to maintain healthy relationships. Being in the church raised my standards for all relationships, platonic and romantic. I probably went a bit to the extreme by blocking many of these people from my past, only choosing new people with whom I felt very safe.

These people generally fell in a very conservative, sometimes radical, Christian community. At the time, I probably needed that extreme change, but later, I needed to calm my black and white mindset back to the balance beam. I felt it was alright to find my change of scenery and to switch things up from the way life was before, but, being an extremist might harden my heart more than soften it, in the end. At some point, the hurting ones may return to the balance beam, finding love for themselves and for others, regardless of trauma triggers.

In order to understand why I made the choices I did, I needed to think for myself without other's convictions and opinions hovering over me, even if out of love.

The group I became involved held the strict standard that either you were believers in Jesus or not, it was very black and white. I could talk and spend time with you, only if we did the following together: spend time together in groups, give side hugs only, talk about Jesus, pray, and have praise and worship during most of our time together.

We disallowed any physical connections, so not to cause any romantic confusion. If any man were to ask me on a date, I immediately refused, thus breaking his heart and deciding he could only be treated like a brother, nothing more. I became extremely shut down to the idea of dating, and thought that for myself to heal, dating these "healthier" men was simply out of the question.

There was a time I began to lead a small group at my Mom's home in Sunset Hills. I invited girls from high school to a bonfire in my backyard. We would meet, I'd have a sermon or word of encouragement prepared for them, and then we'd talk about it. Afterward, we simply spent time together talking and hanging out. It was great! I really enjoy leading small groups!

I was following a DVD series to spark my focus for this small group. One in particular, inspired me to elaborate on facing your fears. I am not one who enjoys being even a subtle hypocrite, so I practiced facing my fears head on! I am certain I was afraid of much, but my two biggest fears at that time, seemed to be a fear of the dark, and a fear of being judged, for being an introvert.

One night, my family was away and I had the house all to myself the entire evening. I decided to keep all blinds open late at night, and walk around my house at 11:30pm. I walked in the dark around my home praying until I felt the fear was gone. After my eighth lap walking around the house, the fear was no longer there!

I had become familiar with my surroundings, so I wasn't swallowed by fear. What we fixate our focus on is what we will become, and I started focusing on the sounds of birds singing at night, the street lights, and knowing that I now had safe neighbors, and a cellphone in my hand, in case of emergencies.

I had to dwell in truth and the facts. I focused on overcoming fear of the dark, and I overcame it! Likewise, I never wanted to feel judged for the time I enjoyed alone.

I always spent most of my time alone, writing, singing, going for walks or bike rides. My time spent alone was good and healthy for me. Many people seek distractions to help them through a hard time, but for me, alone time was the most helpful.

When grieving or wrestling with reality, the silence might seem very loud. You'll know you've conquered your beasts when the silence is no longer a tormenting rage in your mind. When you find silence, you become aware of the hardships you have faced. At this point, you can finally learn from yours, as well as other's mistakes, and then begin to take the steps to grow in the process. You'll learn more about your heart posture, and how you would like to see the shape of your future. As we process, silence turns to peace.

I've spent time alone since I was a little girl. Now, I was in high school and being alone was not very popular. At that age, quantity in your friendships, mattered over quality. I remember how much I wished to read alone at a table in my favorite coffee shop, with a cup of Chai Tea; but I could hardly bring myself to do it, until, *one day…*

I decided to face my fear of people's judgement, and walked into this cafe with confidence. A group of popular girls sat in the cafe. One of them worked there, as her Mom owned the place. I went in with a book, carrying myself strongly to order my Chai Tea Latte, and sat at a table by the window alone. Those girls gawkingly looked at me.

I sat my bag on the seat across from me, showing I was not expecting anyone else, then I read my book and enjoyed my time alone. Maybe the girls weren't even thinking of me. Maybe they were jealous? I had felt so comfortable to be seated alone, and proud to have found it enjoyable rather than embarrassing. I am unsure what they felt, but today was different.

Now, I was able to find familiarity in the dark and in my much treasured time alone. In facing my fears, I found comfort and truth in my identity and introvertedness. I found my self worth. In becoming familiar with my surroundings, and intentions I grew confident, for confidence is simply familiarity with *something,* like a hobbie, talent or a place or person. To be familiar with *something* is to feel confident, safe, and at home.

I've found with men, familiarity wasn't so easy with my track record. Triggers are unhealed wounds. When I would see a man who resembled another who abused me or stalked me, it set off a trigger, and it made me feel unsafe.

A trigger might also bring fear or panic and an antagonizing thought that you'll always be alone, and never understood.

Though I grew in confidence, I was so unfamiliar with the sporadic panic attacks, that I began to resent what spurred on the anxiety.

Rather than becoming familiar and comfortable with fear, I needed to become familiar and confident in what I wanted, and didn't want in my life.

I remember this look each of my male offenders carried. They all began to look alike, with their hallowed eyes with monstrosity features reminiscent of a vampire. Ready to take your life for all its worth and do with it whatever they wish.

Knowing only these types of men like these, I was about to have my first encounter with the extreme opposite of these men. I met men who feared God, concerning hurting or confusing a woman; men who steered so clear of sexual intimacy, that they were socially awkward with girls, rather than perverted and always thinking out of lust.

This changed my view of men as a whole. I was beginning to notice that some men are capable of good, and this allowed me to feel safe while feeling open to dating, or even having a platonic relationship with a man again.

I am very grateful that I am now able to enjoy conversations with almost any man. They no longer scare me, because my idea of men is this: they are not this *alpha person who is always above me, wiser and stronger,* but they are human too, capable of right and wrong. The difference between a good man and a bad man is the temptations they give into

Whether Christian, Agnostic, Atheist or if a man comes along resembling mannerisms and looks like that of a past offender, I remind myself that they are actually not that man. These feelings, this discernment is a warning sign. Right now, I try to be civil to all men, set my boundaries, and not let them into my life beyond those boundaries.

My boundaries are firm, and I wouldn't have it any other way. It is a freeing feeling!

I think a big worry is that abuse and behaviors from men won't stop happening. Truth of the matter is, we will never know what will or won't happen, or how much more pain we'll have to endure. Truth is, we cannot control how people will treat us, but we can control how we respond to situations.

Now I choose to have boundaries, and do all I can to cut off ties with that type of personality or action. I won't go it alone, once I feel uncomfortable. I will get the help that I need so that I feel safe. I will be certain someone knows about my discomfort, so that I can forgive and move on.

When you love well
When you care for others kindly, gently
and with grace and patience,
then something disrupts that peace.
That something brings a tidal wave of control and
manipulation harming you.
Your desire may be to erupt with warning and with a
superhero complex.

I've been there. I've wanted to declare certain people
unforgivable, toxic and ill-equipped to withstand their
destiny or to change for the better.

Stand down. Pray. Forgive.
These people are not worth your time or your energy.
We give more attention to those who hurt us than to those
who love us deeply and wide. The bitter and scared response
stops here.
As I cry forgiveness, many will turn away and say,
"I don't need to, this situation and this person is different;
unforgivable."

Is your righteous anger worth giving up the time you could
have to heal and love? Is your pride worth overwhelming
surrounding relationships because you cannot let go of a
person who offended you?

Sometimes, it just takes God to change and impact hard
things and minds. It takes you to forgive them and yourself
to gain true freedom from the situation and from a victim
mentality.

g u e s t　　w r i t e r
CARI MADISON
(Pen Name)
Liscensed Psychologist

Imagine this: A client has experienced multiple losses in his/her life. They now obsess with prevention plans, however, their actions are not the most helpful, but more harmful. What type of advice do we give to someone with a passion to support people and prevent pain, post trauma?

I met Vivia through a mutual friend. We started talking and connected over our like-minds for people and psychology. I graduated from the university where she studies Psychology.

I experienced a situation with Vivia where she struggled to put herself first, in a very trying relationship. Vivia has been transparent with me from the beginning of our friendship. We've truly helped each other in multiple hard times. When Vivia needed a therapist, or to understand more about her own anxiety and depression, we would talk together, and I would refer her to my best friends in my professional support system. Her strength and boldness, how she acknowledges her self worth, inspires me as much as she says I motivate and inspire her. It's a give-and-gain kind of friendship with Miss Vivia.

Through our many conversations, I learned Vivia was transitioning out of a superhero complex. In this state, a person might try to save people while they themselves are still healing from their own trauma. This can be very harmful to the person and anyone they attempt to save.

Vivia knew she needed to continue to grow and heal more, before trying to help others. I have been there to watch her process through this with more grace than she's expressed she's been able to walk in before.

Layers of trauma influence how we make our moves when helping others. These layers can and will blur lines. In the effort to avoid our own healing, a "Superhero" will try helping others, and it won't work because the unhealed parts will flare and project onto others in a harmful way. They'll have an eye for a population already vulnerable, and will only have one shot to support them, or not. It is important to have a good frame of reference as to avoid hurting those we intend to help. This goes for licensed professional counselors as well. We must heal before we cast our life coats.

A part of being healed is admitting and knowing you are a constant work in process. You're never fully finished healing from trauma, and you'll never be perfect. It's important to continue to do your own work, as you guide other vulnerable people, to prevent blurred boundaries.

Some people struggle with secondary trauma. Vivia has experienced many losses and through one of our conversations, I learned more of how she used to project her anxieties, rather than placing her energy into healing. If someone has anxiety about repeat offenses, or a fear of dying like a friend who died by suicide, or an accident, while nowhere near any such situation, I'd advise EMDR and future template work. It is enriching and healing to simply imagine yourself in that space, where you are no longer experiencing the trauma you've worried about.

Complain or Change

Journal about your like-situation.
Were you able to form change from complaints?
If not, how will you find peace for your heart?

Reclaim Yourself and Forgive

Reclaim yourself and forgive. Forgiveness is a tool we use when we have healed just enough, that we have nothing left to lose.

If you're still angry, it's too soon to forgive.

If you can't show me your scars and tell me exactly what happened to you, its still too soon to forgive.

That does not mean its too late to let go of your villains and reclaim yourself.

If your ready to let it all go, the grief, the pain, anger and trauma, and if you're open to finding out who you are instead of always trying to prove yourself...

then forgive.

A Vulnerable Process

R e m e m b e r :
I cannot be helped unless I want to be helped.

I might always need therapy.

Initially, only I know when I need help and professionals can get me the right form of support.

I have to change my attitude toward failure and being a victim.

All I will experience will teach me strengthen me.

I did not ask for the things done against me. I certainly did not ask my mind to paint and repaint harsh memories as flashbacks.

T h r e e   r e a s o n s   v i c t i m s   f o r g i v e :

1. You think forgiving quickly will make you a good person
2. Victims feel a lot of pressure to forgive by everyone else
3. You think forgiveness is a shortcut to healing

" FORGIVENESS IS SUCH A POTENT FORCE, THAT NONE OF THOSE REASONS WILL STICK. "

Faith & Vision
WE MUST BELIEVE IN SOMETHING

I am a dreamer. I have a few new ideas a day. My ideas are big and vibrant! They involve how to impact people's lives and support people in a brilliant way! Not everyone sees in dreams.   I am multitalented and multi passionate. Not everyone is. I could be an Esthetician, a Nanny, a writer, a full time Mom, a Clarity Coach, a psychologist, a business owner, a photographer. Some do not know what it is they could be.

Perhaps they are not familiar enough with themselves; lacking confidence to pursue an idea. Perhaps there is fear that if they put an idea out there, they wouldn't actually be able to see it through. It is risky, but what if it does work? How brilliant!

Dream with me, so that you might look forward to something. Imagine with me, so that you might feel purposed.

I have the upperhand here because I have faith in Jesus. As a Christian, my imagination is full with the stories from the Bible and Holy Spirit breathing in me that I might love people well and unconditionally. This faith alone, that anything is possible because within my faith, all things are possible, is healthy for me. It encourages me to have vision and find purpose.

What is your belief system? Your world view? What is it in your life that promotes your ability to dream, to imagine and to be childlike?

The Girl Who Cried Forgiveness

If you had no fear, worry or doubt; and if you had unlimited resources including money, what would you want to do with your life? Write it out.

Do not hold back, then consider what it takes to pursue this and dive in.

Victim over Victor

Looking into her eyes
Remnants of pain show fire
The grey that's deep and bold
invites you into her soul
a tiny little dancer
with a mind full of gold
even if she feels blue
butterflies flutter without a hand to hold

she is me and she is you
look into the mirror
into what is clear
you have overcome
and you will be okay

fourth chapter

17 ON WEST MAIN STREET

How can we grow and sharpen our discernment? We need to be aware of manipulation and control, and have accountability to mentors in our lives. I have found having such awareness with people in my circle has protected me from downward spirals, helping me to break chains.

This brings me back to the power of forgiveness. Imagine, chains wrapped around your waist, linking and connecting you to each person who's ever offended you. They are linking you with their lies and judgment from an abusive action. As you try to move forward from the Harperlitating situation, you have to leave the valley where you felt defeated. You must climb out of this pit, walking slowly and steadily, allowing yourself the time to gain self worth, and confidence, all the while moving upward and onward, toward your destined path in life.

As you walk up this steep hill from the place you were bruised, beaten and burned, verbally, mentally, emotionally, physically and perhaps even spiritually, you must use every bit of strength you have within you. This will be even more challenging to walk uphill than ever before. You feel weak in mind and spirit. This, in turn, takes a toll on your physical body, bringing you to feel unable to handle one more painful thing.

You start to melt down, feeling burnt out, yet you must keep going, fighting, and trying to move forward in spite of everything. Remember these chains? They are linked to your offender, until you forgive him or her.

You will carry this person and the situation between you both, as long as you have breath, because if you continue to put all of your energy and time into this situation, it will always remain. You must find resolve, and there are steps to get there.

There is absolutely a need for anger, grief and mourning, but there is no need to live in the situation forever. This person or situation does not have to be a part of your process and future forever. Each link connected to the offender must be cut completely, in order to continue your uphill journey. If ties aren't cut, chains aren't broken, then your offender will continue to pull you back down into that dark pit from which you have tried so desperately to escape.

Example: I have walked up mountains with bruises and wounds, both physical, and mental. I have climbed far to escape reminders of my past. The people at the end of my chains were like venomous snakes. When I ran into a situation while climbing upward, that situation triggered rage, bitterness, sadness, and frustration from my past. My offenders felt like venom in my bloodstream, climbing up my legs, stopping me dead in my tracks, paralyzing me, sending me spiraling downward back into the victim mentality.

After each new offensive attack, I would spiral out of control, camping out in a pit of despair, licking my wounds, trying to hide. Eventually, I would regain the lost ground, attempting to slowly move forward again.

Camping out on a mountain hasn't always been my cup of tea. High on the mountain top, there are different and unfamiliar beasts, and other things that have room to attack countless times. In my weakness and insecurity, I had to learn how to overcome these battles in my mind, for the battleground really is in our mind. I had to begin to forgive.

Each time I worked through this process of unforgiveness, I let go of these people and their power of control over me. Finally, one chain link after the other fell off, shattering to the ground.

I couldn't be reminded of the pain any longer, and in this process, I found a new piece of myself. I cannot forget the memory, but the pain from the memory began to dissipate.

It will be the biggest challenge you've ever faced, to try and walk up the mountain, to find your greatest potential, if you are carrying the weight of your offender with you everywhere you go.

Trudging through the mud, rocks, and hard places, while carrying your offenders with you, they will take all of your time and energy. This must come to an end once and for all. It's an absolute MUST to cut this tie, and let the offender and the offense go. They do not deserve your time, worry, fear, energy or future. They must be completely surrendered, as they are no longer a part of you. You are moving onward and upward!

Consider two situations that you feel you need to forgive, that you're ready to begin forgiving. You get to begin breaking off the chains linking you to the past, and prohibiting you from the future. Your offender is losing their power and losing your interest. You are moving on!

You've been imprisoned by pain, by depression, by frustration, and therefore you are paralyzed. Now the prison door is opening, offering you a way out. Some will stay in their cell, because it has become familiar, second nature, and far too comfortable.

Some will have adapted to this state of mind and continue to stay there. Their offender on their chain link will remain until they realize forgiveness is the powerful sword against the enemy. They are used to carrying this weight around with them, and to lose it would feel strange. This is why many people return to toxic relationships, due to familiarity. This is a cycle many people live in their entire life.

Do you want a new norm? It's time to see what has happened, how it made you feel, and to write out new boundaries you'll have against it, allowing you to finally leave that prison cell you've called home.

The door is open. Will you leave, or will you stay? It's your choice.

<u>Let It Matter</u>

Where does it hurt? Why does it hurt? What will you do about it? Should you do something to impact yourself and others, or yourself alone? Write out your thoughts.

_____

_____

_____

_____

_____

_____

_____

_____

_____

_____

_____

_____

_____

_____

_____

_____

_____

_____

Fourth Chapter

Let It Matter Lyrics: Johnnyswim

*I don't want to feel better
I don't want to feel good
I want to feel it hurt like losing someone should
I'm gonna let my heart break
I'm gonna let it burn
I'm gonna stake my claim with the flame I know it hurled*

*Run baby run
Don't you know I've tried
But escape is a waste ain't no use in hiding
you know the best way over's through
So if it matters let it matter
If your heart's breaking let it ache
Catch those pieces as they scatter
Know your hurt is not in vain*

*Don't hide yourself from the horror
Hurt today here tomorrow
If it's fragile and it shatters
Let it matter, let it matter*

*They say you know it ain't easy
I wouldn't want it to be
Cause ease is for the shallow
But we were from the deep*

*I don't want no distractions
Don't try to please me for one day
You are worth the joy my love,
you are worth the pain*

Limiting Beliefs

We are often unaware of our limiting beliefs because they were "passed down" to us by the attitudes and beliefs of others. As long as they remain unconscious (we are not aware of them) they can hold us back from achieving our fullest potential and experiencing joy. For example, if we have heard all of our life that money is the root of evil then we may unconsciously create situations that limit our financial success out of fear of that evil.

Below is a list of some common "phrases" that we are often told growing up or hear in our community. They are so "normal" that we rarely question their validity or consider how they affect our belief systems or make us unhappy. Of course, there is some truth and a good intention behind most of them, but consider which ones you have been conditioned to believe and how they have impacted your beliefs and your life.

"Money is the root of all evil."
GOOD INTENTION: money does not bring happiness and can corrupt
CONDITIONED FEAR: negative association with having money; it turns you into a bad person
POTENTIAL LIMITS: unconsciously avoiding or sabotaging financial success to avoid the "negative qualities" you believe you'll develop if you have money

"No pain no gain."
GOOD INTENTION: the reward is worth the struggle
CONDITIONED FEAR: the belief that in order to be successful one must suffer
POTENTIAL LIMITS: choosing not to make changes or go for what you want because you feel it will be difficult or painful, holding yourself back from success

Limiting Beliefs

"Finish your plate. There are starving people in the world."
GOOD INTENTION: Don't be wasteful with food and have compassion for others
CONDITIONED FEAR: food scarcity or guilt for having more opportunity than others
POTENTIAL LIMITS: over eating and health problems or holding yourself back to avoid feeling guilty over having more opportunity than others.

"Money doesn't grow on trees."
GOOD INTENTION: be intelligent with how you spend your money
CONDITIONED FEAR: money scarcity; feeling that there is not enough and it is hard to get
POTENTIAL LIMITS: not believing you can have what you want if it involves having money and therefore not going for it.

"Don't burn your bridges."
GOOD INTENTION: keep good relationships with people who may one day be a resource
CONDITIONED FEAR: apprehension to do what you know is right for you if you feel it will make someone disapprove of or reject you
POTENTIAL LIMITS: not making a change or taking an opportunity when it comes out of fear of disappointing, offending, or otherwise burning a bridge

Limiting Beliefs

"Life is hard."
GOOD INTENTION: pain and struggle are a normal part of being human
CONDITIONED FEAR: there is no hope of you feeling at ease or happy in life
POTENTIAL LIMITS: feeling discouraged and hopeless; accepting difficulties or unnecessary suffering because you believe it is normal or expected

"Honor thy mother and father."
GOOD INTENTION: treat your parents with respect and be grateful for them
CONDITIONED FEAR: overly concerned about disappointing your parents or that you will be disowned if you follow your heart
POTENTIAL LIMITS: holding yourself back from what you want and know you need to do or who you are because your parents (or others) do not approve

"No one ever said life is fair."
GOOD INTENTION: sometimes things seem unfair, but it is okay
CONDITIONED FEAR: you will not get what you deserve and there is no justice in the world
POTENTIAL LIMITS: you may hold yourself back feeling like it will not pay off or you may develop feelings of hopelessness

Limiting Beliefs

"Good things come to those who wait."
GOOD INTENTION: it is important to be patient and it's worth the wait
CONDITIONED FEAR: you have to wait a long time to get what you want
POTENTIAL LIMITS: a feeling of impatience due to focusing on the length of time and not doing something you want because it will "take too long"

"You have to pay your dues."
GOOD INTENTION: it takes effort to get results
CONDITIONED FEAR: you will have to suffer in order to be worthy of any pay off
POTENTIAL LIMITS: feeling unworthy, you may not take opportunities or you may punish yourself for rewards and accomplishments you receive with ease

"Speak only when spoken to."
GOOD INTENTION: be polite and don't interrupt
CONDITIONED FEAR: apprehension to approach others or speak up
POTENTIAL LIMITS: avoidance of activities or circumstances requiring you to be in authority, lead, demand what you want, stand up for what you believe, or speak in front of others

"Children are meant to be seen and not heard."
GOOD INTENTION: really, there is no good intention here
CONDITIONED FEAR: feelings of being unworthy and low self-esteem
POTENTIAL LIMITS: avoidance of being in the spotlight or anything that would make you feel important or valued

Limiting Beliefs

Which of these phrases were you conditioned to believe?

_____

_____

_____

_____

_____

_____

_____

Can you think of others?

_____

_____

_____

_____

_____

_____

_____

_____

_____

Limiting Beliefs

Do you believe they are all true? __Yes __No

Can you see any fears you developed because of them?

_____

_____

_____

_____

_____

Can you see any way in which they have limited you?

_____

_____

_____

_____

Can you see how you would be happier with different beliefs? How?

_____

_____

_____

_____

_____

Limiting Beliefs

What are some new beliefs you'd prefer to have instead?

_____

_____

_____

_____

_____

_____

_____

_____

_____

_____

_____

_____

_____

_____

_____

The Girl Who Cried Forgiveness

When you develop your world view, what factors contribute to your chosen perspectives? For example, when deciding to be Pro Life or Pro Choice, have you placed yourself behind the line that saves face, or behind the line that brings confidence and peace to your heart?

If you do not know what to believe in, know what to believe against.

Groupthink occurs when a group of well-intentioned people make non-optimal decisions, by the urge to conform. Group members refrain from expressing judgements, doubts or disagreement within the census. Members may ignore any ethical or moral consequences of their decisions. When groups feel they are physically threatened, or that threats are made to their identity, the group may develop a strong "us versus them" mentality. In some cases, the outcomes of groupthink are destructive.

When times are uncertain, people are eager to find meaning and comfort. Through social and mass media, we are fed much hype as conspiracy theories spread. We are also prone to quick judgements based on our raw emotions, not facts. We must accept what is our truth for the following reasons:

Because I believe it
Because I want to believe it
Because I have always believed it
It is in my (positively) selfish interest to believe it
I believe our world views are not meant to be publicized to make a change, but to lead our own lives in the direction we wish to go privately and morally. On your own, avoiding leapfrog brain, what do you believe in?

The Girl Who Cried Forgiveness

My friend and I went home to Minnesota over Independence Day weekend. She's a very dear friend of mine. She has a heart of gold! Kimmy has a heart for people in a way I've never experienced before. She already experienced a messy family Christmas with me, and now was able to enjoy Minnesota's short summer. This trip wasn't just about us being happy tourists. She wanted to experience more of my background story. As my dear friend, she wanted to be ever ready to provide accurate imagery to the words in this book. She wanted to attend a church service at the place that had shunned me, as well as many others. She wanted to understand, taste and see a glimpse of where I'd spent two years before being excommunicated.

She was upset with me after the service. Her pure heart was righteously angry, in a way that I could absolutely understand. She wanted to have hope for these people, but my stories of how they had hurt and controlled me, influenced her so much that she couldn't feel any love for them whatsoever. The entire experience had her paralyzed and moved to tears.

I've always had a fear of being misunderstood. This transcended into my relationships, and it may have come from that one experience that involved a relationship, where I felt completely misunderstood, and taken advantage of by certain people.

I am now able to see how a crush I had on a certain person in this church, affected me so much. I consider this time frame of the lingering crush to be the pivotal point where I let curiosity, butterflies, and excitement take over my emotions, getting the best of me.

From that high point, my emotions would be led to the polar opposite of being misunderstood, and utterly rejected. I felt that I was being made to look like the creep. May I was overexcited, too involved, but to be made to feel unattractive, unwanted, untalented, unloved, (especially by church leaders) you name it, I felt it. This should never happen to a new Christian.

How much of this outpouring of insecurity came from the

wound burning deep within me while I attended this church?

Why was I shunned by these church going believers of God? Was it their own discomfort and inability to communicate? Was it their selfish intentions, with ulterior motives regarding others? Do the leadership even have good intentions for their congregation? I felt so confused.

After this time at the church, I felt I was dirty, gross, not authentic, due to all they had spoken over me. This is exactly opposite of what one should feel under their leadership at church.

I felt they thought I was dishonest, a target to empty their dirty laundry onto, not good enough, not wise enough, weak, and unable to discern right from wrong or good from evil. In hindsight, I know they were projecting onto me who they were, rather than dealing with their own issues. It had nothing to do with me. I saw them do this to others and it broke my heart. It is very sad to see this continue to happen.

So how can I know if I'm acting out of an old wound, or projecting my fears and triggers onto someone who doesn't deserve them? We always need to be careful to know if we are discerning something off key, dangerous, or if it is something we are projecting. No one is exempt from projecting when they are not healing. If you recognize you are projecting, consider the steps necessary to heal this open wound.

When something is occurring and you are familiar with some of the actions in the situation, you may be triggered. Seeking forgiveness, helps one to find where the pain is coming from, and why it keeps bringing triggers.

Have a person you trust help you to verbalize your feelings. Find someone who knows you and your past, someone who can help you connect the dots, brainstorm, and pursue healing rather than projection.

You might be wrong about a person or group. Past hurtful situations may have taught you *what not to do*, which situations to avoid in the future, but you also need to know the right things to do, in order to accelerate your healing process.

Have you left your own prison cell? This will impact your ability to know how you can discover the influence of your future. I believe that your safety and mental health is worth redirecting any situation.

You'll find that it is simply a reminder of pain, and that you need to dive deeper, in order to obtain your healing. You might also discover that you were correct in your assessment, and should be grateful for any past situations that taught things preparing you for the future. You can now go back and address that situation thoroughly, simply by applying the appropriate skill set gained through the process of forgiveness.

I see many take their pain and sweep it under the rug. I've seen how suppressing their sadness and pain has projected onto other healthy relationships, crippling them. When people are deceptive, conniving, and controlling, their whole purpose is to make their way into your life, leaving you powerless, while promoting themself into a place of total control. We need to step on the head of that snake with our heels, and stomp hard, killing the control.

We must have boundaries. (This is an example of developing boundaries around those people. Put your foot down and keep it there. You will teach people how to treat you; what's acceptable vs. what's not acceptable.)

The offenders were linked to the chains of your past disappointment. Consider they are now leeches and the only way they can stop sucking the life from you is if you pour salt on them. You cannot simply allow the leach to stay, unfortunately you can't be too kind to this *person*. Again, it is their whole purpose to gain control by pushing you down.

Once you've done this, you need to clean the wound/s, allowing it time to heal. Things feel differently now that the leech isn't there. You'll have lost that burden and now you can allow it time to heal. You will need to protect the wound in the healing process with time and space.

Fourth Chapter

I will share how I did this:

I forgave my Dad, I wrote him letters. I stomped my heel on the pain of the memory. For a while, I avoided watching movies with sexual abuse involved, as I embarked on my career in the Psychology field. I will carry these boundaries into my caseload, assuring I do not have too many abuse cases, for it is too close to home. I poured salt on the situation, and that looked like answering my "What If" questions.

What if he was capable of being a loving father now? What if he would apologize? What if my parents could remarry? What if my family would forgive him too? What if my family had stayed together? What if this happens to me again? What if any of this didn't happen? Would my life and relationships be any different now?

When I went down that avenue, I learned he wouldn't and can't be a father-figure for me and that he was non-repentant, I knew I needed to completely let go of the leach and carry on in healing this wound without him.

When this was all said and done, not one "What If" really mattered anymore. He changed my life and the lives of those around me. My next What If question became, "What if I let this illusion go and made the best of my life from here on out? Would others follow my lead?"

What he did, robbed me of sleep and accelerated my fear of man. What he did changed my life forever, and it will not have my future.

We can forgive someone without ever needing to contact them. The power of our imagination is incredible! If we give ourselves to imagining the person is seated in the chair right before us, we can close our eyes, have a conversation with this person and gain closure, freedom through forgiveness and even restoration from the painful memory.

The forgiveness process is amazing! I have not needed my offender's attention or connection in order to forgive him/her. I needed to let go of the weighty memory, and the pain linked to his/her person, and I did that on my own.

I spent six months doing forgiveness therapy twice a week, with a group of women, in a private room from one to three hours. I would be seated before an empty chair, then asked, "Who do you feel you need to forgive today?" The person I needed to forgive, always came to my mind immediately, quickly and somewhat surprisingly. I always thought my Dad was the root of all my pain and unforgiveness but actually, it was so many others.

In my first session, I expected my Dad to be the first one I'd consider when asked that question, but alas, it was a woman I felt most betrayed by, who was the most challenging person for me to forgive. She was first and repetitively seated in that hot seat across from me where I'd confronted her, cried before her and forgave her. My boundary with her is strong. As I noticed my freedom from the pain I felt from her, I realized she will never be one to ask forgiveness from me, and that it is not a healthy relationship for me to try to rekindle. I will be civil with her, I will not share details of my life happenings with her, and I may never even see her again.

Acknowledging the frustration and pain helped me to acknowledge my limiting belief that all women are selfish with ulterior motives. I came to this thought process because of the experience with this woman I had trouble forgiving. She experienced a very similar situation with her boyfriend. The difference between her and me was that she was asked to leave the church and still came back. I, rather, laid down a boundary line and refused to return to this church of *conditional love*. She could have chosen to empathize with me by supporting me, but rather, she too decided that I needed to leave and be shunned.

This forgiveness process introduced my encounter with true and liberating freedom from the person's actions and control I'd given over to them. It was in that room where I'd spent six months understanding the inconceivable power of forgiveness.

<u>Boundaries</u>

Reflect on your life: what are some things that keep repeating themselves (patterns):

_____

_____

_____

_____

Why do they keep repeating themselves, and how could yoU change it?

_____

_____

_____

_____

What are some of the "triggers" that create a negative emotional response in you (words, phrases, body language, foods, actions, people, environments)?

_____

_____

_____

_____

_____

The Girl Who Cried Forgiveness

What are some of the triggers that create a positive emotional response in you (words, phrases, body language, actions, people, environmemts)?

_____

_____

_____

_____

_____

_____

_____

Make a list of 5 things you can do or think in any moment to give yourself a Joy Boost.

1. _____

2. _____

3. _____

4. _____

5. _____

Now, use these positive triggers to shift your emotions to JOY whenever you want!

The Girl Who Cried Forgiveness

Church leaders are not perfect, but human, therefore, capable of making mistakes. Though we may desire unconditional love from leaders and influencers, we must realize that they are incapable of giving that to us, and we are also of giving it back to them. We need to quit expecting perfection.

Though I know there are some good and balanced leaders, some leaders are capable of starting fires to cauterize a wound that's starting to heal, while others might bring about third degree burns. Some leaders won't even pass you a bandage. The variety is too large, and balance is a rare find amongst leaders. Again, we need to quit expecting perfection.

I have talked with many who have served in ministry and I do realize many feel placed on a pedestal. Many give so much to others that they wind up feeling burnt out, thus distancing themselves from the people that look to them most. Honestly, at this point, they probably need a break, but they just keep doing the same thing day after day.

Many leaders require tough skin, because they are hurt by their followers. Just as a doctor takes an oath, as an attorney swears his vow of confidentiality, ministers are also supposed to take their job as a shepherd of the flock seriously. I don't even think all of them do the things they do intentionally. However, when everyone is idolizing you, it's easy to let pride replace the humility you started out with, and the leader you were has changed and is not the leader you are.

If you have a right heart within you, I think God's heart is always for you. Perhaps he still uses manipulative people to support others, perhaps just to give said manipulative persons numerous opportunities to humble themselves, and gain a right heart.

I believe God uses everything and everyone. He even uses the churches full of chaotic people, even after they've shunned many members.

I'm going to tell you a story involving me and a small church. I was the second to be shunned. They would never say they are shunning you, but it's exactly what they are doing.

This is a love story.

With braces and piercings covering my face, a framed short bob hair cut, I smiled at the boy across the room. My friends invited me to their concert. Apparently this charming guy, that I couldn't take my eyes off of, was their friend. I knew the lead singer and that he had purposely invited me with flirtatious intentions, but it became quickly obvious that I only had eyes for his friend.

He had a fair complexion, light eyes and dark hair. I loved how his hair complemented his skin tone, and styled the frame of his face. We were both in our prime that night with braces and quite the apparel, sporting a rocker vibe. I was on a mission at first site, and by the end of the night, I handed him my cell phone with "Add Contact" on the main screen, and he successfully added and saved his contact information beneath his beautiful name. His aesthetics, and the sound of his name, were just a few reasons I was absolutely smitten by him. I was going to be seeing him again.

I didn't expect this response though. We met at a Christian concert, and here he *assured me* that he was a Christian, and didn't think he should be dating.

Mr. Big Shot must have thought me naive, as though that concept was unfamiliar or oblivious to me. Did he think I'd never heard or dropped that line before? Everyone who is a Christian teen knows these are words we use. It implies they are directly from God's mouth, when we aren't interested in a person, and need to let them down easy.

He didn't know anything about me, so his texts seemed to be stereotyping me as a godless child. With a little drama, I let him go.

Our mutual friend had now invited me to lead worship with his band on the beach strip over the 4th of July. We had a lot of fun doing this! One open stage, on the lakefront, offering different ice cream treats and a space to worship.

Ethan, the lead vocalist, invited me to join his family to a two week long worship gathering about 40 minutes from us. I worked it out to go. When I got to this tent gathering, my journal couldn't shut, and my head wouldn't lift up. Writer's block didn't exist here. The theme of this gathering was "Renaissance" meaning *revival of the arts.*

That's just what was happening. I felt everything that had been stripped from me when Dad went to prison was *here.* The arts, the creative people; people who understood my mind a bit more than my Mom's side of the family, came flowing back to me without even talking about it. My constant writing was highly encouraged and creativity was in the air.

My last season had been hard, but now I was coming out of the darkness. My hair was now cut short and blonde. I'd cut it in spite of my Dad. It was a very short fused and emotional decision, coming from memories of my Dad's desire for me to have long and pretty hair. It felt perverse for me at this point, so I cut it all off and it was still colored dark. Now it was blonde and short! I was disconnecting from that wound.

The worship was inviting and the musicians were skilled. I've never experienced God with such devoted creativity by the people in the worship band. Low and behold, the pretty boy from Ethan's concert was there and he recognized me. This time, Jasper seemed *smitten* by me! Maybe now, he would see I was a Christian and not some punk rocker rebel. His stereotypes fell off his mouth this time and he seemed eager and determined to find out more about me. I avoided him, of course. I'd let it go of my crush on him and now, he was doing the opposite, crushing on me.

When I closed my eyes, my imagination ran wild. I could see so much. I'd close my eyes to pray for someone and it was as if God was visually and spiritually downloading everything to me. I would share with them what I saw and heard. If I closed my eyes while writing, it made writing easier as well.

Every time I saw Jasper, I closed my eyes to avoid him. However, this time, I had a vision of him. I really felt God gave me the vision. It was so vivid, and so clear! He was alone by a lake and needed help. He was angry and sad and couldn't seem to part from the anger and sadness. I wrote it down and gave it to his sister-in-law, who gave it to him and said, "A pretty girl wrote this for you." Jasper spent the night trying to connect with Ethan to find out who I was and how to get a hold of me.

The next day there was a writer's group. This was the first group I had ever gone to, and it was incredible! We were given many writing prompts and I thought my pencil might start a fire on its own, by how much I was able to write.

Ethan had a crush on me too, and Jasper kept trying to call him. Ethan knew why, so he wouldn't answer his phone. On my walk to the writer's group, Jasper took matters into his own hands and caught up with me introducing himself. Later he told me his plan was to see my handwriting to confirm I'd written him a word of encouragement.

I learned his parents were the pastors of this church, hosting this gathering. They did this every year in August for two weeks. His walls weren't as high as they'd been before at the concert. He seemed more humble, childlike and sweet. There was no hiding the way our eyes were catching each other's attention. He wasn't really a writer, but came to the group to be near me. I grew concerned as days passed and we grew closer, and he never wrote, but it was apparent he was a phenomenal writer when he put his mind and heart into it.

Jasper was a musician. He played the guitar. These were the simple things I learned about him. Everything else was just a connection. Fireworks filled the sky on one of the last nights of the gathering, and he laid beside me on a blanket and held my hand. That connection is nothing compared to any hand I have held before. We became the very best friends instantly, with so much love for one another.

Jasper and I saw each other often. We communicated constantly and in every way possible. "Good morning" phone calls, texts, and emails throughout the day and goodnight calls until we'd see each other again. This was very much a situation only high school students could keep up with, but it was all joy! We wanted this and we only thought of ourselves at this point. We were happy and determined to spend as much time together as we possibly could.

Neither of us had a car yet, so it was very exciting when we were able to drive. We did everything hopelessly romantic, from going to concerts to coffee shops, watching the clouds and pointing out the shapes of them. We had picnics and walked hand in hand downtown, away from anyone we knew, because *this had to be* our secret.

His parents didn't want their children to date until they were eighteen. We were only fifteen and sixteen. This private romance kept on for two years. From our first set of fireworks to hand holding, to our first kiss, then staying awake all night writing poetry, trying to express this incredible connection to each other, with God and our dreams for the future. He was my very best friend. Then, the unthinkable happened, and all hell broke loose. We had sex.

We were so young and felt so much love in our hearts, but his family was against it all. Our timing of things, our high spirited emotions, the love we felt, pretty much everything about the relationship altogether was coined as a disaster. Because *his family* was against us, the rest of the church community had to side with them, including friends and family.

It was frustrating to feel so strongly about someone, and yet be without advice on what to do, rather what not to do. We loved each other very much, but couldn't express it and had to hide it. How could we ignore this? It became so hard that anger and resentment, love and disappointment became like the child who was told they couldn't have the cookie, and they are going to have that cookie no matter what!

I'm sure to them, this seemed like a juvenile rebellion. However, once we started this relationship and added sex to the mix, our course was set, and there was no going back.

Most times, the sexual relationship was really fun! We didn't care where we were. In a car, in our college locker room or a stranger's bed while housesitting. We only wanted to be together. We did try to stop having sex before marriage, as it was becoming exhausting and the secret was growing vulnerable and about to burst and ruin this relationship. We were in a catch 22 situation.

Easter was coming and the message was "Repentance." His Dad, the Pastor, talked freely about this powerful thing that could set you free! He encouraged people to repent and without fear or worry. I encouraged Jasper to repent with me, but he highly discouraged it, saying he knew what would really happen because it happened to his older brother with his first love.

I didn't listen to Jasper. I was betraying his trust while letting go of my trust for him. I needed to follow this conviction to tell the truth. I hadn't learned secrets to be anything but poisonous. My hopes were to come clean and move forward by getting the help we needed to have a healthy relationship in the future.

I was choking on this, and finally came to the edge where truth was the only option. I sent a text message to his sister-in-law, Blair, saying, "Jasper and I have been having sex".

Our dream world was shaken up!

Jasper and I imagined our marriage, our home, our children, and freedom together. We built a world that no longer harbored shame. Sexual desire built up, because we felt so frustrated. We simply couldn't enjoy each other without being critiqued or dismissed.

So, our alternative, have sex, and it became our go-to stress reliever and the best way of connecting with each other. Our creativity and strong bond once made this relationship fun. Now, it was only exhausting.

I went from a broken family to this big dream of having a wonderful marriage creating a sweet, wholesome family. I was beginning to let go of the idea that he could build that with me.

I imagined the drama that filled his family's house. Every light switched on as Blair walked across the house to Jasper's room to assess the situation. He didn't see it coming as perhaps he should have. I received a mad text from Jasper that night. He couldn't believe I told her. He thought I would listen to him and that I trusted him.

In hindsight, I now recognize everything I already knew. His family was behaving as usual, controlling and manipulative. They were extremely loyal to only one another, and saving face seemed very important for their ministry. I wasn't a part of the family by blood, and so they were loyal to assure no one would know of Jasper's sexual history with me.

My friend Will liked Jasper's sister, Mercy. The Teal family did not approve of Will, much like any other guy she brought around, good or bad. If the Teal's didn't like someone, *then you weren't allowed to like them.* It was about loyalty. Concerning my longtime-friend Will, I was told I needed to choose to stand beside Mercy or him. I shouldn't have been told that.

We should choose people based on love for them. We should not have to choose sides when two people you love disagree with one another. To choose a friend over another, by the demands of a manipulative person, will certainly bring with it a high price to pay.

The cost to love is far greater than the cost of spitting someone out of your mouth in the name of love, for someone else's approval. That is complete and absolute nonsense.

Will's father died and due to *this* families' orderly commands, I could not be there for Will at his Dad's funeral. This played a large part in completely flipping Will's life upside down, with triggers and grief that have lasted a long time. I don't think Will has ever totally recovered from the spiritual abuse he suffered from these people. It's unfortunate that this occurs every day with so many people.

Neither Mercy nor I were allowed to go to Will's father's funeral. Looking back, I can't believe, after all I'd been through, that I fell for that; when I myself had faced so much rejection. However, what one will do to fit in and feel belonging, was exactly what I was doing to feel I belonged, regardless of the cost to me. I had no idea yet how high that cost would be. I felt like the worst friend to Will. I felt stuck and without freedom to just say no to these people, I needed to go to the funeral because he was one of my best friends. I felt heartbroken and most of all, I felt I betrayed him.

I was extremely loyal to these people who only discouraged me. I wasn't encouraged to try new things such as singing or dancing. I had to take that upon myself or be encouraged by other friends in church.

Coty gave me vocal lessons and Carri Ann gave me dance lessons. It was incredible! I didn't want anyone else to know. I didn't want them comparing or judging me, especially to the other singers or dancers. They already had me in a slot and to them, I was the writer and that was all I was allowed to be in their casting of roles and manipulating of people.

I felt I was doing enough to invite others from school to help populate the ministry, by staying in the neighborhood, the community gained value and encouragement. When the Teal's would seemingly become annoyed with me, they would encourage me to go back to my family, though they once told me that being around my family wouldn't help my growth in the Lord. It would be best to stay away from them. I was moved around based on how valuable an asset I was or was not for the family and their ministry.

I watched the doors revolve after returning home from an internship in Kansas City. No one had been pushed out just yet, but at this point, I sat from a bench of hindsight bias.

This internship prepared us to love well. We learned so much in a month, and the largest piece I took from the internship was to love all people who are around and beside you, including those you don't understand. I was able to take that to beauty school and loved all people regardless of our differences.

I met the most interesting group of people in that course. We studied hair, skin and nails. The Esthetics teacher saw my natural abilities in the spa room as stronger than with hair and nails. I later flew with that natural talent. That's where I met Dani.

He was a big guy with a big heart, long hair, polished nails, lots of makeup and a deep voice. We connected when he heard a music playlist of mine during class. I was listening to my favorite artist, Lykke Li. He told me he liked my style and taste in music. This is where our friendship began.

Classmates didn't know what to think of us. I was a Christian and he was a crossdresser transitioning into the biggest decision of his life, transgender surgery from a man to a woman.

Dani had a heart of gold, and I knew he had a big heart for me, as I did him. We protected each other in those school hallways, from stares and judgment. My best friends, Maria and Jasper, attended that college too. They had different majors.

We often ate lunch together. In class, back in the beauty department, I arrived with dark and creepy looking photos of Lady Gaga on the mirror at my station. I found Dani lurking around the corner and giggling. That morning, I didn't have the time to clean my mirror before my first client, an elderly woman receiving a perm. I was so embarrassed, so the next day I put crosses and a Bible verse on Dani's mirror. We played tag like this for quite a while.

Dani opened up his heart to me. I share this with you because he's no longer with us. He was really hurt by men, and when he started feeling a connection to something greater than all of that pain, (like faith in God) something horrible happened to cause him to lose all trust again. Dani died by suicide in 2016, never completing his transgender surgery and never finding confidence or a sense of identity.

In a meeting with the members of Inflame, I let them know I invited Dani, a crossdresser, to church. I felt I had to let them know that someone was coming who didn't look like a person we were used to seeing around our small community. I briefly shared about his experience with much abuse and lack of trust for men.

That being said, I specifically asked that no men pray for him, lay hands on him, or hover over him. I was very protective of Dani.

Though they nodded in agreement in the meeting, they did the exact opposite the night Dani joined me. Pastor Teal invited nearly every guy in the church to surround Dani, laying their hands on him to pray for him.

This scared Dani very much. I could see how extremely uncomfortable he felt. He went to sit in his car, ready to leave. I followed him to his car and apologized, feeling awful and outraged. We continued to see each other in school or at my Grandmother's house from that point on.

Now, I'm not saying its Firestarter's fault that Dani died by suicide years later, but I am saying they were not very sensitive to the real war going on inside his mind and spirit. They seemed much more concerned with themselves and the testimonies they could collect, like trophies. They rather pushed their agenda to the limit, trying to get what they wanted. If attending this church, you best be ready to follow their way, or be prepared to be called weak and wrong.

This was a church of the twenty commandments. The first ten were Biblical, but the second ten were not. They told you what you could and could not do, what you could and could not say, where you could and could not go, and who you could and could not see.

I watched as some people were accepted into the church while others weren't. The good looking and talented were not of question. Those who had skills to benefit the church were absolutely made to feel at home, while others weren't considered important at all, but questioned and critiqued, chewed on and spit out.

Maybe there were people who weren't just like *them*. Maybe they were people attending the church who were just getting to know their spiritual beliefs...it seemed Inflame only wanted the spiritually mature, malleable and talented at this point. The problem with this is a church isn't for the well, it is for the sick, and the body of Christ is to be there to help the sick at all times.

When I came home from my internship in Kansas City, I returned to Inflame. Then, I was accused of harboring false humility at my home church. This made me angry! Why hadn't

Inflame taught me the bible the same as the leaders of the internship had? I was only learning by the church of "The 20 Commandments." My connection to God was judged and belittled by so many once I returned home. I felt in a box, and if I moved confidently in something, I'd be taken outside of that box to have a talk on humility and reminding me of my low spiritual maturity. One benefit to leaving this church for a month, was the ability to see with a different perspective, not so highly influenced by the manipulative breath of my home church pastors.

When Blair, (Jasper's sister in-law, a leader on the worship team), received my text revealing the great repentance, every light turned on in the house. on the way from her and her husband's house to Jasper's parent's house, to Jasper's room.

The Teal family lived in the same house. Two married brothers, one with a child, with Jasper, his sister, and their parents all under the same roof.

Jasper texted me, absolutely pissed off to have woken up to Blair's shocked and upset text message. That's the last I heard from Jasper for a long time.

Jasper's Mom, Charlotte, took my best friend, Maria's Mom, and confronted me in the church building, telling me I should leave. It seemed immediate regret filled Charlotte as I walked out of the building. I knew by her words, "Maybe this isn't right, I don't know! Maybe she'll come back in a year and be with Jasper?" Why would I come back?

I drove to a lake access nearby and let my heated and sad emotions out in a loud scream, scribbling down this poem "I Am Spring". Next, I called a friend I had in Kansas City, who was already concerned about my loyalty to this church from the beginning. He encouraged me to come back to KC for healing. He made many valid points, and I wanted to do nothing less than be far, far away from this maddening place immediately.

Out of the blue, a policeman showed up at the lake access, where I had a panic attack, and was then brought to the hospital. Mom, Grandma, sister and brother were there. Some journalists from the local newspaper came to my hospital room wanting to know details. Still, my loyalty was strong.

I kept my experience to myself as I attempted to catch my breath in my brown paper bag, and didn't leak who had sparked this panic. My brother didn't hesitate to text and threaten Jasper if he ever talked to me again. Charlotte called me and asked if I was okay, and to see if my loyalty was to remain as someone helpful to the ministry. To avoid being a burden, I answered kindly and protected her, as I replied, "I'm fine."

Why did I go to Inflame? Why did I stay? I went because my initial introduction reminded me of my Dad and his creativity. I was reminded of the good memories concerning my Dad at this place. I felt I could restore my creativity by being surrounded by like-minded people in a *healthy environment* called church. While church can be a healthy environment, this church environment was not healthy for me. I had to come to that realization and remove myself.

I stayed because I fell in love with the Pastor's son. I stayed because I was convinced that if I left, I'd have nothing. I began to feel uneasy about my attendance, as friends expressed their discomfort when I invited them.

My Uncle once asked me why I liked it so much. He noticed that I gave much of my power and reason over to these pastors. In my response to his questioning, I admitted that while recognizing the people had issues, the true reason I stayed was to find my connection to God.

My Mom once told me I wouldn't be allowed to attend any longer if I came home crying my eyes out again. It was then that my eyes began to be open to the truth. I was staying in my own prison; it was an addiction.

I became comfortable with staying there, though the door was open wide, waiting for me to leave. I couldn't leave, and I wasn't sure why, but it was starting to become clearer to me as those around me who loved me gave their input. I finally started to listen.

Fourth Chapter

When I responded to the Pastor's invitation to transparency, I was hurt. His promise of restoration, healing, and support, was not awarded to me. I finally recognized the control, deceit, and selfishness that had been there from the very beginning. In hind-sight, this was a church with many cult-like tendencies. Unless this church could publicly give an apology for how they hurt me and how they've hurt many others after me, I could never recommend anyone attend this small ministry. They are attractive, they are good at creating and marketing new concepts however, they have ulterior motives once you're a part of the ministry.

I do forgive these people, but I think we always have to be aware that there are wolves in sheep's clothing and we are to be protective of others and expose those that would hurt the innocent.

As I said before, Blair was the hardest person for me to forgive. I still think that might be the most challenging situation for a victim of misunderstanding to have. People who can truly understand your situation, and empathize with you, then turn against you completely.

Blair did just that. I think the difference between her and me is that she decided to go back and marry into this family. I couldn't find the desire, loyalty, patience, or wisdom in my entire being to ever return to Inflame.

Fourth Chapter

Now, my days at church are very different. I have more freedom, and I avoid being in a leadership role at present. I choose which spiritual leaders I attach myself to, as well. My convictions are not the same as everyone else's around me, but we can still find it in ourselves to give and receive love.

I attend church to develop my personal connection with Jesus for who He is to me. He is who I choose to believe will never leave me, never forsake me, never abandon me, never manipulate or control me. It was the people I couldn't trust.

They are incapable of perfection and true humility, making decisions with ulterior motives because they are human. They will cheat you, push you down to get ahead, lie to you and use you. I couldn't follow man's lead completely, but I can follow an invisible King and His Word, who propels me forward to be a good human being.

I now attend church because if I want to. I do not attend church for community; I have community elsewhere and everywhere. I do not attend church for people, but for my personal relationship with God.

Since beginning my studies in Psychology, my mind has grown and my definition of unconditional love has become true to the true sense of the words put together. If you've heard me pray in the past, my prayers sounded like, *"Lord, I pray you would make this person just like me, so that I am comfortable. Let my will for them be Your will so that I can be comfortable around them. Amen."* Do you know how much I hate that my heart posture mimicked that?

Everything in me desires to have an authentic, non-codependent Christianity. Everything in me hates religiosity, and churches of the ten commandments. I will continue to call myself a Christian, because that is who I am, a follower of Christ. I refuse to act as many Christians, going to ministry school, yet only ministering to their peers in the program, fearing spending time with certain people because they don't want to become like them, or gain bad influences, and-excommunicating people in the name of Jesus... This is wrong!

Jesus is a man of unconditional love, who would spend time with anyone of any nation, tribe, tongue, and I believe, belief system. I do not wish to be like Christian leaders, or my peers, as I wish to carry those characteristics of Christ wherever I go, and in whatever setting.

I have a tattoo on my forearm that says it all. In the times of pain and tragedy, people couldn't help me. Through the power of my imagination and the words in the Bible, I knew and believed that, "*I am not a burden to (Him) You, I am the rose. My weaknesses cannot intimidate (Him) You; You call me the Lily.*"

No more collecting "Saved" quotas, living in blind loyalty, or a bubble. I am free in Christ and He actually lives in me, whether I attend a church, have Christian friends or not. Either you live by being a Christian or you don't. If you have a relationship with God, you feel a sense of belonging, whether a member of a church or not. God's love is simple.

"UNCONDITIONAL LOVE MEANS TO LOVE WITHOUT CONDITIONS. MANY WHO STRONGLY ADVOCATE FOR UNCONDITIONAL LOVE STILL MANAGE TO LOVE ONLY THOSE WHO BELIEVE AND THINK IN THE SAME WAY THEY DO. IT IS MY GOAL TO LOVE ALL WITH A TRUE UNCONDITIONAL LOVE"

Even with churches I deem *healthy*, I have my boundaries. I forgive and have grace for the Pastors and their leaders, as they are human. I personally feel uneasy when I think of ever singing on a worship team, or leading a small group in the church. It's so damn political now, I cannot tolerate the critique or criticism inside the church's four walls. I also cannot imagine the pressure I feel to always be so perfect. Many churches seem to have built a shelter meant to protect and love people, yet many rooftops and walls only keep the attendees appearing as though they are spotless. This can be so harmful. This can make one passive about the things they are doing that are not healthy, ethical, or up to such a moral standard.

With the umbrella constantly covering you, speaking life over you, one can find it hard to get away from that, to even hide for a few Moments. The church or Christians can camouflage truths about you; the church becomes your crutch, letting ego take over. The painful thoughts and actions pursued under the radar go unnoticed without being recognized.

This is very evident as I consider pastor's and deacon's kids. By the nature of their parent's roles in the community and church, they are looked at as pure, innocent, told to hold the standard and never sin and that's a lot of pressure. The protective and proud shelter built around them often becomes a bubble, where they intensely rebel, due to a lack of freedom to mess up.

When too much pressure is applied, they explode! They burst! They rebel. Some do it outwardly, and some inwardly. Either can be dangerous. Of all places, I wish the church would practice more vulnerability and transparency. As of now, it's not there, or it's too extreme, to the point that no one can have privacy or a good day.

guest writer
WALT MEYER
Music Minister

I have been a Christian since 1971, and have served in various paid and unpaid roles in the church. I have served in many capacities of the church from worship leader to youth pastor/evangelist. My main gift is as a music minister, graduating from Christ For the Nations in Dallas, Texas in 1981. I was ordained in 1983 and then again in 2015. I met Vivia through her friendship with my wife, Julie. Vivia and I have spent many hours talking over various topics over the years and stay in touch to this day.

From Vivia's experience within this chapter, I would encourage Pastors, who have previously offended or hurt someone in their church, to deeply consider that when we hurt someone, typically they begin to accuse us of doing something harmful to them. They tend to tell others as well. This creates a lot of unnecessary negative emotions and drama for everyone. Jesus shares a rather unusual piece of advice in Matthew 5:25 that is hard for most people to understand.

We must admit that when we hurt someone, we have done something wrong in their eyes. We need to recognize their pain. They may have exaggerated the situation, maybe misunderstood some details about what happened, but regardless they feel hurt. If we humble ourselves, agreeing silently in our hearts before God, that there is some truth in their accusation, then that posture creates an atmosphere of reconciliation. As a church leader, we should always be pursuing reconciliation.

If we can come to a reconciliation, then the accusation

can be laid down and aside from the healing that takes place, our own reputation is restored. Love must look like something. It must lead to Christ and His example, and I believe a part of that example is forgiveness.

If you are a leader who was hurt by "the church," I would encourage seeking out help. Find a safe and healthy sounding board, like a counselor, psychologist, or a mature friend; someone unbiased. Talk about what happened as it will help you to move forward. It's healing to share your story with someone "safe", especially when with a heart that wants to be healed.

I know someone (in ministry) who experienced a deep hurt from his pastor. This pastor was calling his wife and told her to divorce her husband. She was told her husband was jealous of her ministry and would ruin her ministry. After a few weeks, his wife told her husband what their pastor was doing. He was so angry and shocked. He quit going to that church. One day, when he was home, the pastor called and the man answered the phone. He told the pastor to never call them again or he would call the police.

This man ended up going to a doctor and was diagnosed with clinical depression. He started taking a prescription for this, but it didn't help much. He would think about different ways in which he could kill that pastor. He had trouble sleeping.

He was a believer, and had been to bible college and had been on a staff member at a few churches. He knew he "had" to forgive this pastor. He would pray about it but nothing changed about the way he felt. He even felt guilty for having anger towards that pastor.

After about a month, he was praying and asking God to help him forgive. Out of nowhere the hate left him and he actually felt sorry for the pastor. He asked God to help him love this pastor. After about a year, whenever he thought of the pastor he only felt compassion for him. Eventually, he almost forgot about the situation.

This man didn't tell anyone about this pastor for many years. It would have helped him if he could have, as long as that person was able to truly help him learn how to forgive.

That man was me.

Later, I learned that my depression was caused by my repressed anger and bitterness. The more I wanted to hurt that pastor, the worse the depression got. The drug only masked my feelings. I didn't know that there are other RX that work quite well. I was able to function without the RX so I stopped cold turkey. Please don't do that either. If you need a RX to move forward for awhile, then find something that works. Don't be ashamed, like I felt.

I began to pray blessings on that pastor. I was sincere. God helped me. God's love is a powerful force and it empowered me to forgive and find healing. I would rather be at peace and feel compassion for this pastor than to hate him. This is a choice, and it is a place of power!

I struggled to want to go back to another church. We moved a couple of times, eventually finding a church with a pastor we got to know very well. We moved again, and this did not hurt our relationship.

Over the years, I have been tempted to gossip about that situation. I have learned to control my thoughts and tongue. That is the evidence of the life giving power of the Holy Spirit. So if you have been hurt by someone in the church, please find one or two mature people who are unbiased that you can talk to. Your ability to deal with the pain and issues will take some time. Forgive yourself as well, for feeling guilty and hateful. Give yourself grace to heal.

Your anger, at first, was actually healthy. We are created

to defend ourselves and anger is an emotion that helps with that. But unresolved anger quickly turns to bitterness and then, potentially, a mental disease. You can see yourself as the victim if you want, wallowing in self pity, or you can see yourself as a person who is going to overcome and forgive. There is a pure power in forgiveness!

As you forgive, you will find yourself being more guarded with people. That's OK! Guard your heart with great diligence, for out of it flow the issues of life. Be wise as a serpent! What does that mean really? A snake is very protective of its territory. Even a rattlesnake will rattle its tail to give the intruder a warning to leave.

It's healthy to not fully trust any human being. It's sad when we don't trust some leaders. Trust is earned. We can honor imperfect people and leaders because it shows a respect for their position and humanity. Our safety line is to know we are not required to trust immediately.

God has so lovingly forgiven us all of many terrible things. If we really believe this and will receive that forgiveness, then our hearts are free from shame and guilt and can be focused on learning how to love even the most difficult people. In this process you will find it's OK to take care of yourself too. Love looks like something. Forgiveness is the proof. Release your anger and hate. It is only hurting you and not "them". Let His love wash you and feel the power in that. Freedom from hate is a very powerful place.

It's worth the effort to learn how to forgive. The old chorus is right, "He paid a debt He did not owe. I owed a debt I could not pay. I needed someone to wash my sins away... and now I sing a brand new song Amazing Grace! Christ Jesus paid a debt that I could never pay".

Fourth Chapter

g u e s t   w r i t e r
ZACK HENSLEY
Pastor

I am a Senior Pastor of New Hope Fellowship, and a Bible College Teacher in Elim Bible Institute in New York.

I met Vivia when she interviewed for a camp counselor position as I directed the camp. I learned of her heart, and saw how much healing God had brought to Vivia's life. Her heart is amazing, considering her history. I remember a moment where people were sharing different testimonies, and Vivia shared her story. At the time, it was obvious sharing her story was a little raw in it's delivery. It was not a time for her to share yet, as she was still healing. I remember encouraging her to take time, to really finish the journey first, before bringing others into it, due to the harm it could bring to herself and to anyone listening.

In hindsight, Vivia remembered how many people wanted to sensationalize her story. This was the first time she'd really been invited and encouraged to take a step back. I encouraged her to take time to heal fully, so that she could share her complete story of redemption later on. It is incredible to see her move in this now, and in a way that sharing such personal depth heals her, and invites others to do the same without harm.

I also saw Vivia in the process of recognizing, and then trying to cope through an unhealthy relationship. A lot was being asked of Vivia that was unfair in the process of wedding planning. My wife and I were her premarital counselors for a few sessions. Her personality and dreams were no longer prioritized by this family she was meant to marry into. Some of the things asked of her were because of what happened to her in the past, and this caused her much pain. I watched Vivia process through this, and find her value, over this unjust sacrifice. She found her self-worth again, and released herself from this relationship.

There were many situations where Vivia found herself a victim of an unhealthy relationship, even with the church. An unhealthy church is a church where anything but Jesus is at the center of focus. In unhealthy churches, the pastor, leadership, giving or the mission of the church becomes the main focus, but not Jesus.

My goal, as a pastor is that I would be there to serve people from where they are, and to Jesus. I am a custodian, serving people, assuring they have a safe and healthy place to come connect with Him.

We get off sometimes and try to draw people to us. We want our church to be a bridge connecting them to God. If not, it's unhealthy and that's when the church becomes cult-like and that bridge may collapse. Success in a ministry or church is not by size or finances, but this one equation: Did the people get closer to Jesus and His word? If so, then it is a successful church, if not, it is an unsuccessful church.

A church has to be honest, and about Jesus, it is then that they are genuine and authentic. People are looking for hypocrisy: anytime a person presents one way when leading, and another when not leading, this is hypocrisy.

We must seek authenticity. Are the leaders of those churches truly after Jesus, or something else? If the church is about money, success and greatness, it gets found out in the decisions they make, and even the people they hire. You can always pinpoint the unhealthy things based on the pursuit; Jesus? Money? If not of Jesus, you'll see a ton of unhealthy fruit.

You might see leaders fail and make bad leadership decisions, but if they represent a healthy, whole body of

Christ, you will see their pursuit is Jesus and their faith. Some healthy churches may not handle everything correctly, but that healthy church still stands on their feet in a healthy environment because of their pursuit of God.

I would encourage anyone who fears returning to a relationship with a church, to give themselves first to the pursuit of a relationship with Jesus, putting themselves back out there, even if it hurts.

Take it slow and one step at a time. Do not volunteer or jump into teams straight away. I equate this to being in relationships with people. There will be churches to break your heart, but should you ever date again? Yes. Keep moving forward as you would in any relationship- treat it the same way you'd treat someone who had their heart broken.

Take time, heal, don't accelerate one to sixty, but take steps to pursue a new relationship. A church hurt you, forgive them. No one church is the same way. There's another fish in the sea for you! Like a heartbroken person from a romantic relationship makes us weary of dating ever again, we are still after love so we eventually find our way back. If what we wish for is Jesus and to be surrounded by like-minds, we will find our way back in time.

Consider the churches you're experiencing. Are they about Jesus or anything else? If anything else, then move on. Like you would move on from a guy if he's just about sex or hooking up; assure his core and foundation is good. go slow and see what they are about. If it's real and healthy, it'll be good. No relationship will ever be without bumps, disagreements or fights, but at the end of the day, no church is perfect and if their pursuit is Jesus, it will be good!

Tattoo

"I am not a burden to (Him) You,
I am the rose.
My weaknesses cannot intimidate
(Him) You;
You call me the Lily."

fifth chapter
20 ON METCALF AVNUE

You've been climbing this mountain with determination. Everything within you says you are headed toward something "new and better". Your ambition is to live a life wherein you finally feel comfortable and safe. It hasn't been easy. Every time you thought you did your part to find healing, healthier relationships, new rays of hope, once again, here it came, this tidal wave of demons passed. Your same old "Achilles heel" always returns to do its damage once again, finding its way into the same wounded places, scuffing up your knees, bumping your shins, and bruising your heart for everyone around you to see. As you neared the peak of this lingering attempt, it felt as though snakes slithered around your ankles just to pull you down. Pulling you down to a state where you feel helpless, alone and lonely.

People encourage you with their uncaring, passive thoughts, like, "It's going to be okay, this too shall pass" or "pull yourself up, stop crying and get over it." When I'd hear these comments, outwardly, I would smile and say thank you, while inwardly saying, " Leave me alone. You know nothing about me. I don't know you at all. Who are you to tell me this will pass, that I'll get over it." I would thank anyone close to me by saying,

"Thank you for being so supportive and patient of my process. You've been such a good friend." Maybe this was sarcastic, but it felt like sound and concrete from where I stood, as I was giving myself permission to tread water.

It's never another's responsibility to say what they feel is correct, or supportive to someone who has had unfortunate circumstances. Rather, it's up to the victim who was perpetrated to choose how they wish to immerse themself in the best way for them to overcome, and the things they need to do this.

You'll know what you need once you commit to positive psychology and your newly found ability to draw boundaries, and apply problem solving, you will see the peak sooner. Some will know what they need but won't apply it. I needed to leave Minnesota and heal with a change of scenery. This move wasn't understood or encouraged straight off, but I knew I needed it and so I did it. This has been one of my best decisions made.

My friend Steve shared this with me as I cried on his wife's shoulder when I was 20-something-years-old. They picked me up and packed me up after I cried that I'd just had enough. Enough with the manipulative, selfish, controlling and enough with feeling misunderstood and like I'm always needing to change! Just when I thought I was coming to a place of stability and clarity, it all washed away by one person's ability to tamper with my mind and other's perspectives of me. My ex-fiance's Mom had ideas about me and for me that she wanted to maintain. She loved me, she wanted me to be a part of her world and once I showed interest, she decided I needed to obey her every wish and command in order to stay there. Her love became conditional.

Steve called this "The Snow White Syndrome." When people do not have and see what they want in someone else, they'll do anything in their power to get what they want and when they want it. They'll cover their tracks and appear as a victim or always in the right. They'll even cry and manipulate every situation until you might fall for it. These people are famous for gaslighting the innocent. Following suit with Steve's creative explanation of such exploitation, this is something that a jealous person does. I can't quite come to grips with it as I feel indifferent about jealousy.

To me, jealousy can be a good thing! When I feel green about someone's ability to sing well, I do not find it in me to avoid that person, gossip about them or put them down, rather I learn that to have a talent like singing, is worth something to me. So, I decided then that maybe I should try voice lessons! Jealousy tells me what I want in its own way.

Jealousy is good. Jealousy can lift us up and illuminate a true desire of our heart. If we disallow jealousy from showcasing a dream or desire we carry, it can evolve into envy which is even more challenging to rid of. Envy might tag along gossip over this person, bitterness and disrespect.

This just isn't what everyone's default is. I wish it would change. Then pride could be a positive thing and not something haughty and destructive. Then when jealous, we find a gage toward what we might be desiring and do what it takes to obtain it. I'm jealous of someone's financial state? I ought to do everything I can to obtain such a stature by working hard and gaining wise counsel. Catch my drift? I've had enough with the people who act so selfishly and step on people in order to bring themselves up. No thanks!

Alone and Lonely

You might decide that people do not like you
You have broken trust, built walls, stung hearts...
Your words are frozen as they are spoken
As cold as ice, as thick as thieves
And this is how you're remembered
That one emotional breakdown
Maybe you had grounds for your white knuckle fist
and clenched teeth
When did you last breathe?
When did you decide that you are so weak?
Where is the root of all your loneliness?
Dear, how can you conquer it?

But what if it wasn't entirely your fault or your fault
at all?
What if the blood was spread from other's hands,
Only rubbed onto your skin?
What if "they" are all you've known to never leave you
Disappoint you, confuse you, hurt you
Bruise you, and the emotional marks remain
Are you at fault still?
When did you last breathe?
When did you decide that you are weak?
Where is the root of your bitterness?
Dear, how can you conquer it?

Fifth Chapter

Moving to Kansas City is one of my wiser choices made. I wanted to heal and I wanted to carry peace about me. I couldn't do this in Minnesota where everything happened and memories stained buildings and seasons. Have you ever heard of "Minnesota Nice"? What that means is to be kind at the surface and passive aggressive. It wasn't easy for me to dig deep into my breaking heart in a state where everyone pulled themselves up by their bootstraps rather than admitting they need support then going to get it. I'm proud about my decision to move away. I left something new from the air to the people, the mindset and the manner, into a space where I could receive healing intentionally.

I did not have the financial means to support myself, really. I stayed with my best friend Maria's family-in-law for a while before finally moving into an apartment with three spectacular girls! None of us knew how rent would come in, but it did. For me, I prayed it in; I asked then received all I needed, to the last penny!

MATTHEW 7:7-8
Ask and it shall be given to you;
seek and you will find;
knock and it will be open to you.
For everyone who asks
and he that seeks will find;
and to him that knocks,
the door will be open.

The Girl Who Cried Forgiveness

At this point in time, I wore sweatshirts and often hid my face in the shadows of its hood. I didn't like small talk, I didn't really want friends. I wanted healing ministry to start and I wanted to bury my past deep down and far from me. I slept during the day and went to a local prayer room by night. In that year, with those roommates, I lived for the rollercoaster! I slowly came out of my hooded sweatshirt and began enjoying the fact that no one knew my past. They did not know me as the girl molested by her Dad, the tattle tale in school or the one always a victim. They saw someone who left home to get help and start over. They saw a dancer, singer, writer and adventurer!

Twice a week, I met my prayer and counseling team in a side room within the prayer room off Red Bridge Road. I was introduced to the power of forgiveness there.

By day, I laid by the pool without sunscreen. Depression held onto me and danced with my eating disorders still. I'd ride around the city, in the passenger seat with one of my roommates, smoking a cigarette just to feel something. I felt numb from all I privately experienced. The burn from the sun and the smoke from the cigarette made me feel alive simply because it made me feel something. Some nights, I wouldn't sleep. I spent it with like-minded Christians longing for peace and showing up for it to happen. Waiting for peace to finally erupt all the ugly that had previously happened.

The girls lived in an apartment just across the street from what we called "The Guy's House". We would collect canned food or something else edible and cheap to bring over for potlucks often! There, we ate! Because everyone pitched in, we could! We played music and found joy together. One-by-one, my roommates and I walked across the street bringing our laundry and borrowing their vacuum. They would come over for writer's groups and other small groups. We had our own little community and it was brilliant! One roommate began dating one of the guys. She was a hopeless romantic, a beautiful bohemian doll face.

After much time of flirting with friends to see what might

go beyond platonic, potlucks, library runs and midnight fun, we'd become quite the family of lost souls. We made the most of what we had in our little neighborhood. At the apartment was a playground that would become overwhelmed with kids once school was out. We met the kids outside and played with them together because their parents weren't doing it. It was special!

This is when I pursued singing the most. I was dating a guy who was tutoring Justin Bieber. He and I lived in very different worlds from Hollywood to Kansas City, and we made it work. He made me feel a princess and I seemed to help keep his humility. My friends began calling me *Hollywood* as I'd walk down the sidewalk to my apartment with heels announcing my entrance. From a date in the city, I walked the sidewalk to my apartment, into my friends playing games together and laughing, I'd go to my room and sit on my deflating air mattress to change into something more comfortable and return to my reality of this gun-shot neighborhood.

My roommate and her boyfriend were growing more and more serious. It was fun but I was protective of her and didn't trust any guy with her. Carson was a new character. He had a past and I loved his present but was nervous about his future. When he was talking about bringing my roommate into his future, I felt protective and on guard. One day, he saw me at the prayer room and felt my tension. Though we'd sing together, make jewelry and hair pieces for friends and with friends together, I still didn't feel I could trust him. In the prayer room, he said to me, "Keep your hair down, love will find you. Come sit by me," A strange thing to say, I thought. He then said, "Can you forgive me? Forgive me for everything? I want to marry her. I want you to approve." I gave him a yes lacking confidence and hugged him. A couple days later, it was announced that Carson had been hit by a drunk driver at some stop lights and was hanging on by life support. My roommate sat in the passenger seat and had left the scene with whiplash. Carson was about to propose to her that night, with the ring in his pocket. This was the first time someone close to me, a friend, had died.

One of Carson's songs played in the prayer room and at his funeral. It was a beautiful song called "Father of Lights". My roommate had shared that days before the accident, Carson professed his love for her then said, "If I had the option, I'd go to Heaven. I love you, but I would love to be in Heaven." Maybe he saw it coming. Maybe Carson did have a choice while in his coma.

I didn't take his passing well. Keeping in touch with my now very distant and numb roommate, I began to wither away myself. Forgetting to take my thyroid medication and forgetting to eat. I'd cry myself to sleep and question God on repeat. My sweet friend Julie Meyer offered me a nice break. She offered to pay for a hair appointment so I could be pampered a bit before heading home for a break from new harsh memories in Kansas City. When I went to his hair appointment, I asked for their best hairstylist. This woman did not practice a proper consultation with me and long story short, fried my dark and healthy hair from shoulder length to a bleached and fried pixie cut.

I felt empathetic now for those losing their hair for medical reasons. I returned to Minnesota on the day of my friend's Dad's funeral. There was an entire community of people who had shunned me from their community before and I would have rather seen them looking strong, healthy and happy. I came insecure, having gained weight and lost my hair and my friend Carson. When I took the attention off myself, I learned that sadness became empathy for my friend as he grieved the loss of his amazing Dad. When I stopped camping out in a victim mentality, I grew empathetic for those who lost their hair and feel insecure by it. The feelings are real and they matter. They need to be felt.

I have read about inner beauty making your outer beauty shine. Up until this point, it never sank in. When we find our inner beauty and allow it to shine, we are next able to accept our outer beauty without pride but with self-worth. I'm not encouraging a bad haircut, I am encouraging taking a break from what is in the way of you connecting with your inner beauty.

I lost my hair. I lost my friend. I moved back to Minnesota when I said I wouldn't. I knew that I needed a change of scenery and that's just what I got. I had returned to a town about two hours from my family, and all else familiar. I lived on a resort and found this empathy driving me to support women who carried insecurities that I had. I pursued beauty school and when home in my cabin, I went through the process of accepting my identity, and finding contentment in the hard things. This took a lot out of me, and instilled much gratitude and value for myself all at once.

I decided that because I wanted hair, I could simply buy it. My wig came from Hong Kong three weeks after I ordered it. Until then, I wrapped scarves around my head and wore hats. I woke up early with my cat, Marketa. She watched me and supported me as I took my first look in the mirror once I rose from my bed. I inhaled deeply before facing my reflection. This would be a continual reminder that my hair was gone, as was Carson, and so was my pride. I looked myself in the eyes and exhaled, "You are beautiful no matter what. God, grant me the ability to see beauty from the inside."

Showering was so hard for me. Running my hands through my hair usually sent me to be seated on the shower floor, hands drenched by soap and snot, mingled with the tears I had just cried. Next, I'd dress and play with my makeup. My weight had fluctuated so much, because of all that had happened, I wasn't keeping up with my thyroid medication. My weight gain was higher than ever before. I could hardly recognize the person I saw in the mirror. I became desperate with post-it notes and stuck affirmations over every mirror and window to cast a reflection.

At this time, the Discovery Channel had created a show going through the Bible. It was powerful! Especially when they reached the story of Samson. I could understand that feeling and this story forever-more. My hair was cut and I felt my strength was gone too. Once my hair was gone, I dropped to my knees and couldn't recognize my strength. This bad haircut was probably one of the best things to happen to me. It's helped keep me in check so that I wouldn't become too attached to my outward appearance, more-so than my heart posture. I was falling in love with myself again, seeing value. Once the wig came, I rocked it for a while, before finding I didn't *need* it anymore. I was regaining my confidence under the circumstances. I was processing *through* my losses, and gaining enough strength to *overcome* them. I couldn't have done this by pulling myself up by my bootstraps.

"THE WEAK CAN NEVER FORGIVE. FORGIVENESS IS AN ATRIBUTE OF THE STRONG."

guest writer
PHIL BOHLANDER
Liscensed Psychotherapist - EMDR Specialist

I met Vivia as a client. Vivia has written many blogs in relation to our sessions pursuing EMDR Therapy. While a Psychology Major at Avila University, and referred by a mutual friend, Vivia came to receive EMDR being both educated and prepared; without filter. Working with her has not been too difficult. Her transparency helps her healing journey extremely well.

If a new client has never heard of EMDR or Brainspotting, or is only vaguely familiar with either, then in the session, I will do a tutorial on the origin of both. I then talk about my experience, which began in 1990 and includes over 30 two-day EMDR special applications workshops.

Francine Shapiro PhD, who developed Eye Movement Desensitization and Reprocessing Therapy was my teacher. I have also participated in Brainspotting classes, including a 5 day intensive with David Grand and 5 other participants. I am certified in both EMDR and Brainspotting.

I explain that although EMDR started out as a trauma therapy, there are numerous applications that are about enhancing skills and performance in a variety of areas. Not solely trauma.

I have also used Brainspotting for unresolved grief and events that are not traumatic but still stick. I look for those who are open minded, like Vivia, and interested in finding new ways to address issues that, thus far, still influence the person in spite of past experience with therapy.

If a person is hesitant or unsure at the time, I will take

that as a "no". I always seek to make sure the client feels safe. Another factor is dissociation. If a person has a history of serious maltreatment in childhood, I am careful to assess for any form of a dissociative disorder. I will address childhood experiences first and often will incorporate hypnosis and ego state psychology.

Vivia was already familiar with EMDR and very open minded. She also exhibited a high level of resilience based on the history she provided. There is no hard and fast rule about how a person will respond to EMDR, and one will not know how fast things will go until actually doing the processing. Vivia was in the small group of those who responded well.

No specific form of therapy is 100% with all people. I have had clients where EMDR or Brainspotting did not work at all. In some cases the client moved on, and in others, clients would tell me that they wanted to "talk" and not use Brainspotting or EMDR. I am always happy and ready to provide counseling instead, and usually it is very helpful. I have had clients who were shocked at how quickly and easily the processing went. Sometimes the client is not aware of how something from early childhood affected them and the rapid surfacing of something can be disturbing. This is not memory retrieval, which is unethical, but rather something they knew but had put on the back burner. I have had clients repress emotions, or abreact, during processing, and would have to pull them out of it, which I always do.

EMDR and Brain Spotting are powerful forms of therapy. Vivia has experienced a lack of night terrors, less threatening triggers, and was able to quit taking Xanax. That was a goal of Vivia's set upon our first session. If you know your worth and what you want for yourself and out of a session, you will be amazed by how incredible it will work for you!

EMDR Superheroes

I closed my eyes and walked into the shadowed memory. By my therapist's facilitation. I was asked to imagine my team!

I imagined that I'd called this team to a board meeting. Here, the wildest of people and characters joined me to tell me they were for me. The people who came to mind were Wonder Woman, The Rock, Vin Diesel, Elastigirl, Pastor Zack and Psychologist, Carron. These people made eye contact with me and told me they were on my team; here for me to battle against all of my shadows!

Out of the board room, my team followed me. We went to Minnesota, back to the white house with black shutters. We went into my parent's bedroom late at night. I experienced myself lying down in-between my parents in the bed with my brother asleep on the floor. The traumatic memory inches closer to the moment my dad placed his hand on my inner thigh-

BOOM! Before he could, Wonder Woman broke down the door and -CRASH!- ran into the bed to pick my dad up by his neck! She pinned him against the wall and then made eye contact with me. She told me I was not alone, she was here now and everything would be okay. She spoke affirmation over me and my innocence and purity. She then cussed out my dad for his thoughts and attempted actions. Wonder Woman swept me up and she hugged me. She took me to safety and she cared for me.

I couldn't imagine my EMDR Superhero's any differently. The power of imagination is brilliant. What we fixate our focus on is what we will become. Through this therapy, I retrain my thoughts. If my mind is directed or swept up by the shadows, I imagine this team. The power of our imagination is wildly strong!

The Girl Who Cried Forgiveness

I've also created a metal storage container. In my mind's eye, I bolted this container shut with floating written words like, "Fear, worry, anxiety, lies, Jezebel, false sheep, unsupported, a dreamer and not a doer, etc." Now anytime more shadows attempt to bring in new written words, I have access to a vacuum that will suction these feelings into the storage container. They are gone and then I become invincible again.

The power of this is beyond me. I even felt a headache once I reached home from my appointment. The headache lingers today (the next day). I relate this to working out and feeling the throbbing of a muscle not stretched in too long. I have done work and it is good and helpful.

Our imagination is powerful. What we give our time and energy too is important. We can forgive people and experience freedom! Then what? We must then strive to find more peace by gathering our team of literal and imaginative support.

Honestly, I was terrified for a moment before my psychiatrist led me through my first EMDR session with him. I wasn't sure if I could relate what we were about to do with my imagination, to a positive or negative experience of mine.

POSITIVE EXPERIENCE:

Grieving the loss of my best friend was very hard. I hit the stages of grief and wasn't sure if I'd graduate any closer to functioning out of shock again. I went to a weekend seminar where people led "Encounter God Sessions" utilizing your imagination to connect with God in ways you haven't before. It was powerful, it was beautiful and good. Maria's husband shared just what happened the night she died by suicide. I am so visual that this memory has been locked in my mind's eye. As if I was right there with him as it happened, witnessing it and never able to unsee this. I wanted to remember our good times together laughing and making weird faces at each other while dancing to 13-year-old Justin Bieber love songs. In this session, I imagined myself with God and with Maria. I could see her smiling, childlike and happy in a new memory. This is my new default memory of Maria. I'm looking forward to how EMDR will desensitize the negative memory absolutely.

NEGATIVE EXPERIENCE:

I was engaged (that's a chapter in my book!) and it's a great thing that he and I are not married. More-so, due to the connections his family and I did not have together. We clashed on many things, especially how we connected with God. I went away to wedding plan and work without distraction of my then-finance. I went to Minnesota to be with family for three whole months! He and I thought we'd move to New Zealand and so this was quality time with my family before the big move. While I was away, I hardly heard from him. In hindsight, I see why. His mom google'd bullet points of Jezebel traits and was quick to decide I fit the list; that I was seductive, manipulative, controlling and more. When I returned to Kansas City, I thought I'd feel excited!

The Girl Who Cried Forgiveness

My body knew before my mind could process, that I was about to be in danger. As a collateral, I had to either experience Spiritual Warfare Healing Ministry, or I could not marry their son. I tried. What they did, was they brought me to the negative experience with my eyes wide open. The facilitator would look in my eyes searching. Always searching for the alleged Jezebel spirit residing in me. We made it all the way to the molestation before the facilitator called out Jezebel. I began to cry and was terrified! As if I was in that bed again feeling my dad's hand on my thigh, my thigh muscles twitched. I couldn't believe they thought this healthy and helpful. I had to get out no matter the cost.

Imagination is powerful. What we feed our minds; what we fixate our focus on is powerful.

Discover the type of therapy that is absolutely essential for our healing hearts and minds.
What support do you need? How will you have it? What does it look like? For me, I experience EMDR Therapy and it is highly effective.

A Crazy World

You feel the sun comes falling down
On this world not simple
A crazy world
You feel all the stars have gone
Blackout; a crazy world
You feel real danger
But you're strong, you know how to get out

Don't give it up because you don't understand
Don't hold back, stand tall, let your walls fall
Because you don't understand, don't give it up
You're big enough, but you don't understand
A crazy world, even in your crazy world

Your feelings falling down
You know you'll catch it
You feel real passionate
A crazy world
Blackout; crazy world
You feel real danger
By yourself, by them and
so much past inside your present

This world isn't simple
But you're strong
You know how to stay out
While keeping in
This crazy world, crazy world

sixth   chapter

21 ON HOLMES ROAD

Seated on a comfy couch near Lackman Road, where my wedding venue was to be, with pillows at my side and on my lap for comfort, my knees were quaking nervously as I looked blankly at the floor. I avoided eye contact with everyone in this room. They called me "Jezebel" everytime our eyes met.

When people fixate their focus on the good, then the good gets better. When people fixate their focus on what is evil and bad, then that too shall be just what they see. Our perspective and perception of things feeds off our experiences, creating our world view. I became a person in these people's small minded world. Their focus was on what is evil and they didn't even realize it.

Perhaps the reason I got caught up in this was my thinking that God is good and will always protect me by shutting down what isn't good. This isn't always the case; God is always present, always a rock and firm foundation to reflect with, meanwhile

"WHAT WE FIXATE OUR FOCUS ON IS WHAT WE WILL BECOME."

people are human and are capable of manipulating without knowing.

My mind has always been curious. I've been a dreamer, a poet, a creative and a girly-girl. This was appreciated by Everly, a woman I met when I moved back to Kansas City from Minnesota. She reminded me of my Mom. At the time, my Mom and I didn't see eye-to-eye. I wasn't thinking *right,* or being wise, as far as she was concerned, I was just someone to be concerned about. She loved me, but our quality time lacked any depth. Everly walked like my Mom, with a body-build, laugh, and tone of voice just like my Mom. I liked this about Everly, so we would go for walks and I'd help clean her home for extra cash. After Everly met me, when I came to her house with a friend, who'd been seeing Everly's husband for mechanic support, she and I kept connected. I was in financial need while pursuing Advanced Esthetics at a Kansas beauty school. She let me use her van for an entire season, so that I was no longer codependent on friends to keep my attendance perfect. I was so grateful, but she wanted more. She never let it rest that she wanted me to date her son. She thought he and I would make a great couple! I said no, and that I wasn't interested in dating anyone at the time.

I gave her that answer a year before, when I was a camp counselor where her son was also working. The camp director had encouraged us to spend our time there for the kids, not for our love lives. I took this seriously, and made it my focus to love on my campers and lead them well. Everly wished I would focus on becoming a part of her family more. After camp finished, I went to a cafe with my friend. Seated at a table to catch up and write a bit, we were interrupted by a fast paced invitation to Maine. Everly called and said, "We are going to Maine. I'm buying tickets in 5 minutes. Do you want to come? You can write there! Call me back and let me know." I am obsessed with the ideas of the East Coast. I would like a tiny home there, to be able to retreat by the ocean for writing as I please. She knew this. I was excited and able to think it through in her 5 minutes offered.

Everly would go to Maine with her husband, her son, daughter-in-law and she had already paired me off with her single son. I avoided this fantasy of a romance this far. I thought I could hide behind my laptop just as easily there. So I called her and said, "Yes! I'll come to Maine with you. Thank you!"

In Maine, we canoed, played board games, went hiking, four wheeling, sailing, went to dolphin watch, and were hopeful to catch whale sightings. It was a dream of mine to experience all of this! I went my own way for some writing once a day.

However, the plans for the trip did not leave much room for writing. She made sure there was plenty of time for me to be alone with her single son. The two of us in a canoe, the two of us in the middle seats of the car, the two of us four wheeling, and the two of us seated on the plane. Of course we talked, found connections, and mingled. This was exactly what she was hoping for. Everly was so thrilled to see me growing more fond of her son. I wasn't so upset about it myself. As I got to know him, he was growing more attractive to me and had a great sense of humor.

When we returned to Kansas City, things began to shift. He and I weren't officially dating yet. I wanted to check my heart, and find if I truly liked him, or if I was only connecting with him because he was who I had to talk to, and happened to be a guy. Was this feeling platonic or romantic? There really wasn't much room to think on it as his Mom put so much weight into the romance.

I remember her stern conversation with me that previous winter. She drove a few extra blocks before parking at our destination, just to tell me how upset she and her husband felt. They'd supported me so much during school, yet I wouldn't go on a date with their son.

I had no clue she was making a bargain with me. It wasn't what I agreed to, still she had it set in her mind that I was to become her daughter-in-law. In her mind, she has supported me since she met me like an orphan in Kansas City. She took it *that* far and it wasn't fair to me.

It wasn't all bad. I really enjoyed most of my time with this family, until I found myself living with them, and engaged to her son.

Not the dress I would choose but just what Everly wanted. Quote: "I had no clue this was the bargain. It wasn't what I agreed to, still she had it set in her mind. I was to become her daughter-in-law that she supported since being like an orphan in Kansas City. She took it quite far."

Have you ever felt something you've called your intuition? You could just feel that something was out of sync, off-key, and not quite right. The sympathetic and parasympathetic nervous systems have opposite functions. The sympathetic nervous system stimulates your emergency "fight or flight" response, all while the parasympathetic nervous system stimulates the rest. My intuition, (that sense of knowing) within my sympathetic nervous system was unable to keep me in the state of resting.

After her son proposed to me, things got sour very quickly. Our sex-drive grew as stress did too. This was how we thought to cope with the dominating control and manipulation pushing onto our relationship. Sex doesn't resolve issues like you think it does, though sex does make you vulnerable and draws you close to one another. The core problem is still there, lingering until you communicate, fix it, and then the problem is solved.

My creativity and my writing was critiqued and questioned as satanic. Everything from my posture to my weight, my muscle mass and diet, my decisions to continue taking thyroid medication my doctor prescribed at birth, was all up for question, concern, and critique. Everly wanted me to fit a specific mold before marrying into the family. My weaknesses were no longer cute, or funny. I was to enjoy cooking, learning quickly, or surely her independent and capable son would starve. I was to stop taking thyroid medicine, and listen to my fiance's Mom's unprofessional advice. Everything they planned for me, as I transitioned as the new wife and daughter-in-law, left me crippled badly both physically and mentally.

Physically, I could not breath normally, unable to walk as quickly, or even sweep floors without feeling exhausted. I literally lost my voice for two weeks, for months, figuratively I didn't have a voice concerning my opinions or choices. I felt like a broken down horse.

Their comments made me stop writing as much. This wasn't who I was at all, but instead, I spent more time in the gym and shaping up, becoming who they wanted me to be for their hobbies. Everly even questioned if I was truly molested by my Dad, or if I made that up as well.

Even before the engagement, Everly felt the world was coming to an end. As a hyper "Doom's Prepper,"she planned to convert her family's mind into her own personal anxiety, and drive everyone to make sense of moving to New Zealand for protection. I was game for moving, because it was an adventure, and a new experience. I presumed that at some point, I could maybe detach my fiancé, Charlie, from his Mom's boob, and start our own life.

Charlie and I went to Minnesota for a much needed break. Things were feeling out of control and we needed some time alone. We went to the cabin in that small town I lived in, and spent time with my best friend, Maria, and her family. The whole drive there was interrupted by phone calls of my fiance's panicking mother, making us promise that we would turn around if she said so, because the end of the world was near.

Most of our long drive was silent, until interrupted by her calls. We tried lifting the awkwardness in the air by reading our fun premarital book. We were talking about where we'd have our engagement photo shoot. I was trying to soften his inherited fears of the end times.

Again, it is my understanding that God is good. Regardless of where we are, if the end times occur, the same thing would happen all across the world. New Zealand would not be the exception, and we did not need to fix fear of this conspiracy theory. We needed to learn to love and not worry. Charlie went from anxiety to regret about ever leaving Kansas City.

This trip was not the break I hoped it would be. Alone with my sweetheart, was meant to be "our time," catching our breath, building each other up, but instead, we had a third party with us, and I did not want to be on this trip with Charlie, his Mom (on the phone) and me. That was never the plan.

In one of the phone calls, Everly grew frustrated learning

that our trip was not taking us to save or condemn my family for their lack of christianity, but to spend time alone and with friends. She was livid and disapproving. As an adult, do you have to tell your parents the details of your every decision? I didn't think this was normal.

Being that Charlie and I were planning for an extravagant move to New Zealand post-wedding, I moved to Minnesota for three months. I was then able to work without distractions, spending time with family, preparing for my wedding, and "the big move." During that time away, I rarely heard from my fiancé, unless he wanted to talk have phone sex. I went with it, because I felt that to be engaged to him, I needed some communication with him over this time. He only answered his phone in the evening while in bed. Otherwise he never reached out to me.

That night, I had my bachelorette party. My girls reserved Vivie's Boutique, a lingerie store, where I was able to privately shop with my girls. Each bridesmaid bought an outfit. I fell in love with the whites, baby blues and pale pink colors! My desire for a cute, romantic, playful, sweet night of making love to my husband, was completely destroyed in my phone call with him that evening. Charlie once had a porn addiction feeding his fantasy of sex with me, and sex toys, while wearing red and black lingerie. He already started treating me like a piece of meat. It was not cute, playful or considerate. As a matter of fact, it's downright degrading.

Sexual relationships should be fulfilling for both partners. Sex positions should be made consentually, mutually, and out of respect for the other partner. The idea of sex had been distorted for me, since I was sexually abused as a little girl, and now, I refuse to follow suit with such narrcicistic expectations.

I can tell if someone isn't authentic, and this shuts me down. I often found sex as a stress relief act, or pleasure only, for the man. The intimacy was not mutual, it was not this "into-me-see" intimacy bit, rather, it was hurtful, empty and always lacking any fulfillment. Sex was only a man masterbating inside my body.

The Girl Who Cried Forgiveness

It was the last of my three month stay home in Minnesota. On my way back to Kansas City, I decided to spend Christmas with my Aunt and Uncle, at their home near Minneapolis. My fiancé met me at the airport. I did think I would feel more excited to see him, when I picked him up from the airport, but our lack of long-distance communication changed that for us. I saw him, and faked my excitement.

On the drive from the Minneapolis airport to my Aunt and Uncle's home, Charlie was more focused on city traffic, than talking to me about how he missed me during our time apart. It was a quiet drive. It was our default to always have sex when we were stressed, and so once again, as usual, that's what we did. Sex was our coping mechanism. On the drive back to Kansas City, Charlie finally said what was on his mind.

On the drive home, out of the blue, he asked me what I thought of counseling. I reminded him that when I moved to Kansas City the second time, it was intentionally for 6 months of counseling. So, I reminded him, "I absolutely believe in it." I thought it was a very odd question from someone who supposedly knew me so well. He seemed relieved by my answer.

After settling back into my routine at home, a couple days passed, and I was told his Mom didn't think we needed premarital counseling. I already booked an appointment with one marriage counseling couple.

Charlie didn't like it when our counselors told him straight up, that his Mom was very controlling and that he needed to support me better. It was then that Charlie decided we wouldn't talk with these marriage counselors again. He never asked me my opinion, he just decided.

I thanked this Pastor and his wife for his time. I continued talking with this couple privately. Now living in a house full of girls as time led to the wedding, I introduced a local premarital marriage counseling couple to Charlie. Again, a different route was suggested. He asked me to trust him and since he was finally trying to lead the relationship, I thought I would. I didn't know his Mom was behind this the entire time.

Apparently, while I spent three months in Minnesota, Everly spent her time online, researching anything and everything she could find about the Jezebel Spirit. She decided that I had the Jezebel Spirit.

My sympathetic nervous system began its twitch. She found a bullet point list of Jezebel traits and said I had each of them. Everly proceeded to call my Mom, telling her I was possessed by a selfish, seductive demon.

Everly was projecting so much fear upon everyone, especially her son. She convinced him in order to save me, and marry me, I would need her counselor, Harper, to lead me through "spiritual warfare sessions". Charlie bought into her crazy theory, focusing completely on evil, and never leaving any room for truth. From that point on, they made my life a living hell, making it a point to call me Jezebel, anytime my eyes met theirs. Their comments were demeaning, cruel, and untruthful. To be honest, they were outright lies. It's a wonder I am still a christian today. When a group of people you trust, start calling you evil, it can be most damaging, causing scars, that never heal, and never go away.

When Everly would feel sick, she would tell the family it happened after I hugged her. I was at a loss of what to do. Everly made it seem like my Mom, who hardly had a relationship with God, believed that I had the Jezebel traits too. Charlie and I passed Lackman Road, the exit to our venue, The Thompson Barn, on our way to spiritual warfare sessions, with her counselor, Harper and her husband. They served out of their home, which they called, "My Father's House" where she often performed exorcisms.

Here I am, seated on a comfy couch near Lackman Road, pillows were at my side and on my lap for comfort, while my knees quaked nervously.

On our way to this session, we passed our wedding venue. At that point, in seeing the venue, I wanted to be excited, but it only became a building I'd see enroute to these spiritual warfare exorcisms.

I looked blankly at the floor, avoiding eye contact with everyone there, because they always said they were talking to the demon inside of me, but it certainly felt like they were calling me "Jezebel" anytime our eyes would meet.

My knees shaking, my hands sweating, my gaze on the floor, and my mind racing, I just wanted to scream and leave. If I looked scared, they would say Jezebel was scaring the unhealed, little girl in me. If I looked strong and unafraid, like I made up my mind to leave this house, they would say Jezebel was prohibiting me from experiencing true freedom. They said they were calling for Jezebel, who was within me, not me, but a spirit inside of me. It was hard for me to believe that they weren't calling me, Vivia, Jezebel.

Charlie came with me to my first few sessions. I remember sitting on that couch with the counselors seated in front of me, the wife closer to me, and her husband standing behind her. Charlie sat across from me, and on the right side of the room. I was then instructed to close my eyes, and allow myself to imagine the night in my parents' bed when my Dad molested me. My hands were on my thighs, before moving to my knees. I was thinking of so many things from disbelief in my current reality, and of the venue that was once a happy place.

My hands moved up and down my legs, removing the sweat from my palms. Suddenly, I felt and even saw a vivid cramp in my right thigh. This is the same part of my body my Dad first touched and squeezed before molesting me. I freaked out, opening my eyes to escape this imagining. I saw Harper and Charlie's reactions, and I felt trapped.

When a person closes their eyes for a while, then opens them, their pupils dilate as they adjust to the light. It was dusk, still the light in this room was brighter than when closing my eyes. Immediately, Harper, her husband, and Charlie gasped, pointing at my eyes saying, "Do you see that? Do you feel that? Jezebel is here. We need to get her out!" Charlie was shaking, believing everything, while I felt overwhelmed and even more sure that there was no demon residing inside me. The cramping in my right thigh felt like an act of witchcraft.

Soon after this session, Harper and Charlie were having a three way call trying to decide what to do with me. By the time Everly left the conversation, Harper told Charlie that Jezebel could enter into his body through sexual intercourse with me. He grew up believing this crazy talk from his mother. Charlie was shaking on the drive home from this session. In this phone call, the three of them decided it best for me to carry on in sessions without Charlie present, but only picking me up and dropping me off.

After the session where my leg had cramped, Charlie and I left for home. In the car, I was telling Charlie how uncomfortable I felt with this process, and that I would rather see the referred local marriage counselors. He got out of the car as I finished talking. Obviously, he was thinking about something else. Charlie's eyes began to water. Without saying a word, he sighed and walked quickly from the car into his parent's house, where he fell to his knees and then admitted to his parents that he and I had been having sex and he was afraid this meant he now had the Jezebel Spirit.

This is not the first time I have been called Jezebel. Back on West Main Street, when shunned from the church, I was even called a wolf in sheep's clothing. How much of what is written in the Word is taken to extreme measures, to be used against people and is more harmful than is supportive?

When people take the words from the Bible literally, division comes flowing in, and the love of God is experienced as conditional. This makes me so angry. I find myself very protective of others who are called wolves in sheep's clothing, or accused of carrying the spirit of Jezebel. If someone is manipulative, controlling, or doing wrong, they require support and help. Would you agree with me that the most angry people appear as the most depressed? While the most depressed people are often the most angry? These people who are actually angry or depressed are more-so than not, projecting their own pain and shame onto healthy and innocent people.

A ministry posted signs of influence by the Jezebel spirit. As I read this article, I was grinding my teeth and my brows became furrowed. Sadness crept through my emotions, as I recognized this as a memory of my own, and something many are having to deal with on a daily basis. Anyone is forgivable and needs love.

It is small minded and harsh to name call. When you call out negative qualities in others, do you not look in the mirror first, to see if you are projecting? When we are infuriated with someone else, it might actually be jealousy, or a reflection of what we are carrying. The reminder off-sets us into fear, that we might become exposed.

The church did not want me to tell others not to come there. They did not want anyone to see them as controlling and manipulative, so they name-called me, and others, who were bold and confident. Likewise, Everly was struggling herself. Fixated on the darkness, she only saw and felt it. She was projecting her unhealed wounds onto me, especially when I stood up for myself.

Jezebel Traits

1. Refuses to admit guilt or wrong
2. Takes credit for everything
3. Uses people to accomplish their agenda
4. Witholds information
5. Talks in confusion
6. Volunteers for anything
7. Lies
8. Ignores people
9. Never gives credit or shows gratitude
10. Criticizes everyone

These signs are apparently seen in those professions to be saved, but do not operate according to the fruit of the Holy Spirit. It is said that because you are under the influence of the Jezebel spirit or the religious spirit, does not mean you are possessed. The words and actions of those at "My Father's House" did not treat me as though I wasn't possessed. It was messed up, and constantly contradictory.

These are signs that someone needs support, or better yet, needs to learn coping and people skills. For those of you who looked to this list and decided someone inhabits each trait and is indeed harboring the Jezebel Spirit, I would say to you, "please sit down, look yourself in the mirror, and learn to love this person, rather than imploding their every flaw."

The flaw that you see in them may not even be real, but only your perspective. Unless you have a plan, or resources for them to receive good support, you need to keep quiet.

Those with the Jezebel Spirit are usually vindictive and if you cross their path, they will come after you. If you have this spirit, you need to repent and allow the Lord to deal with that stronghold in your life. If you don't sit back, you won't be able to answer God's call in its fullness.

It was as though they had researched EMDR Therapy and winged it with a spiritual twist, fixated on the demonic. She fixed me tea, sat me comfortably on her couch, and had me look her in the eyes as she looked deeply back into mine, while bringing me to my memory of the night I was molested by my Dad. When I felt that tight cramp on my right thigh, seeing its indent and wanting the session to stop, I was told that if I were to stay, then I would become free. What I felt, was if I were to become the woman Everly wanted me to be for her son, and for her own gratification, then they'd say Jezebel left.

Instead yelled, defending myself saying that I didn't want this to go on. Charlie was in the room, and said he couldn't believe his eyes. He said he saw Jezebel yelling through me too.

It was me! The girl crying and wanting to be somewhere was me and not a demonic presence trying to withhold me from freedom. I was sad to hear his reactions. This was the man who was supposed to love and protect me. What the hell was he letting these people do to me? Why was I not enough for him? Why did I need to act a specific way for him and his mother? My identity felt stolen and I was captive. I was swayed to be everything but honest and true to who I am; a creative, poetic, girly-girl who is strong, ambitious, determined, and ready to bring positive impact!

Later on, I was told I wasn't yelling at Jezebel or Satan enough or the demon would have left. The counselor showed me Youtube videos of people taking authority over their demons, and told me I needed to do it that way. This was ridiculous. I believe in a God who knows me. My God knows that this shit scares me, and does not bring me peace or comfort and so I will shut down. I did not connect with God in this way, so surely, God wouldn't have me yelling. That's not who I am, but this is what these people needed to see, to confirm their beliefs.

Time carried on as Harper and Everly continued to blame any fall, sprain, or cold on my giving them a hug, or simply by my presence. I was usually highly complimented by my eyes and authentic smile. Now, I couldn't bring myself to form an authentic smile, or to even look up in anyone's direction. I couldn't feel angry about all of this because they would just call me Jezebel. Any hint of frustration, someone would look at the other before coming to me, looking deep into my eyes, "She's here! Can you feel that? Your pupils are dilated. That is Jezebel!"

This was the bargain: I'd continue counseling, or Charlie wouldn't marry me. Once Charlie felt enough shame and fear from this, he broke down and told his religious parents that we had sex. Immediately, it was Jezebel's fault. She was the seductress, and the one who was ruining the entire family, depleting her son from a healthy body. Of course, no room was made for genetics or true health concerns, given by a doctor, nor was my fiance's sheltered addiction to video games, or porn noted in any of this. It was me, I was the culprit with the demon.

Charlie would have his Moments where he'd hear me, recognize me, and love me again. He offered another break for us; we were going to Colorado to breathe. This quickly turned. The same week we were to move into our apartment, where I'd nest and we'd soon begin our married life, but instead he took his parents to Colorado. He and his cousin came to the apartment, I was so happy and imagining the decor of this space. I was happy to imagine a life with more boundaries, and with a better expression of love! My dreaming was interrupted by Charlie telling me I was no longer coming on the trip. I'd taken off work, but he immediately traded car keys with me, so that I had the one that lacked their house key; so that Jezebel couldn't come into their home to infect them with inner demons, once they returned from their vacation.

This is when I stopped talking with them. I had awful nightmares. I was experiencing hypnagogic hallucinations. I was asleep, but not entirely, and the images I'd been dreaming, were too vivid, and disturbing. During this time I limited who I talked with. I had enough of people's opinions, and accusations of me. People who had a good view of Charlie and his family, wanted me to be optimistic. Others wanted far from the drama, and others wanted to support me, and have me end this with him. It took me a minute. I was in a bad state, sleeping on a mat, with an air mattress, without any money for food, and having to choose when and where to drive, because I also didn't have money for gas.

I was so grateful for my best friend, Maria. I spoke with her and the couple who were Charlie and my premarital counselors, now my mentors. I was the only one who'd show up to our sessions while engaged, because Everly believed we only needed these spiritual warfare sessions, and not premarital counseling. I was stuck. Maria ordered Hyvee groceries for me online, from Minnesota, and had them delivered to my address. She ordered all my favorite things and showed her support, love and sympathy. My friend Lyn and her family supported me as well. She felt this relationship wasn't that great from the first time she saw me around Charlie. She said I was not my bubbly self when he entered the room. She let me use her son's car when Charlie later took his back. She and her husband also got me a job at a country club in the area, and helped me get off Charlie's family's phone plan, and into my own bank. She is a nutritionist, who also helped heal my body back to health from its anorexic state.

When bad happens, there is always good trying to protect us. In all of this, I gained a back bone, I learned to stand for myself and learned to develop a strong foundation that no one could sway. I knew who I was and know who I am, and no one can ever gaslight me ever again.

Are you familiar with gaslighting? I received so many mixed messages between Harper (the spiritual warfare counselor) and Everly. It was exhausting! As my backbone developed and I saw myself leaving Charlie, I finally stood up to his Dad. Everly was even called the Sergeant when the kids were little. She always wore the pants and liked it that way. Sean was quiet, and let it happen, while following suit. Out on the deck, I looked at him and yelled. I yelled that his son was missing out on a good man, because he lets his wife rule their entire world. I told him, in no uncertain terms, that he needed to stop being so passive, so that his son could learn how to be independent, and not so fragile. Sean was quiet, and leaned against the railing of the deck, staring off into the distance, as if anything I said meant something, but because of Jezebel, he'd take it as a grain of salt.

I was gaslit by these two women. I was manipulated by psychological means into questioning my own sanity. Imagine you're in a room with someone and this room is brightly lit. As time goes by, the person you're with starts to tell you that something is wrong with you. In your right mind and confidence, you respond that you feel just fine and everything is actually okay. They aren't happy with that response. They argue to say that you are erratic, and not listening to them. This person begins to dim that bright light and tells you that you are dimming the light. You know your hands are nowhere near the light switch, but you begin to see the light dimming. You can't see that they are dimming the light, but somehow as the light dims, and their accusations grow, you begin to question yourself, your sanity and you or the truth. You now believe that something is wrong with you, and that you are capable of bad and possibly even cruel things.

Between Harper and Everly, I was gaslit to believe that there was a demon controlling me, and that because of it, I was a harmful presence to anyone around me. Harper had explained to me that Everly was jealous, and that this would be my best chance to be strong, and leave this relationship. Charlie was not strong enough to stand with me, and Everly wouldn't stop controlling me. She hoped I'd end the engagement. At the same time, she thought Charlie had a chance, and felt he did truly love me; she felt that things could actually change if we were to marry, as long as we stayed away from his controlling mother and passive aggressive father. I knew better, and was reminded by my premarital counselors, that the marriage does not change a man or a woman.

Since I'd broken off the engagement, I hadn't seen Everly

or her family for months. We planned for an April wedding and I hadn't talked with her until that September, 2016 when my best friend died. Everly knew Maria, and I knew I wanted someone who knew her around me. It was strange to hear Everly share her perspective of this spiritual warfare situation. She'd said that she and her family were consistently warned to keep away from me; that this demon wasn't going anywhere, and that Charlie would be in submission to this Jezebel Spirit, causing a lifetime of hardships. Harper and her husband told her I was not submitting to this healing enough for it to work, and that it would be a travesty for their entire family.

While I was encouraged to hope for Charlie, and see his love for me, build boundaries against Everly and her family, they were fighting to stay away from me as a whole. Harper would come back saying there was no doubt that Everly loved me, and I believed that, but then followed it with the idea that it was Everly who had this Jezebel Spirit, and that's how she recognized such characteristics in me.

This was not wise counsel. This was not professional, wise, nor sane. This was a messed up game of people pleasing, influenced by "He-Said-She-Said " gossip. Everly had hoped Charlie and I would try again. At this time, she decided it was all Harper's fault. However, the person to critique me and control me was the one who called me Jezebel first. I could not trust her. He and I met, and concluded there was so much of a mess, that it could not be repaired. He then pressed me to avoid writing about his family and sharing any of my hardship with mutual friends.

A writer is the sum of their experiences, and these experiences are unfortunately nothing new under the sun. Things like, even this situation, happen all the time. People need to know they aren't alone. So I find value in sharing my story, still respecting forgiveness on all sides, and giving all a second chance by changing their names.

I forgave Charlie, Everly, and Sean. It was easiest to forgive

Charlie. He was victim to a codependent relationship with his mother. His Dad never stepped up to support him as a man, so under his parenting, Charlie remained a little boy, too afraid to stand up for himself. I had pity and grace for Charlie. I forgave Everly, because she seemed to walk with a savior complex. Most of the time, she was selfish and manipulative, but we became friends, because she had a sweet demeanor and a desire to help others. Still, she needed healing. Acting out of her savior complex, she prematurely tried to help others. With her own wounds remaining raw, she became (toxic poison) that would hurt many. I forgive Sean for leading Charlie as he did, sheepishly and scared, but I do have hopes for him to change.

Balancing Act
Positive Psychology

Positive Psychology is the study of what makes life worth living. It is considered, with well-being, "the good life". It is the scientific study of positive human functioning and flourishing on multiple levels.

Many people disagree with positive psychology. These people might be extremists unable to see that hyper-optimism is not the fruit of positive psychology, but rather to overcome hardship and shift your perspective as to impact your mental state wealthier. As a Positive Psychology advocate, I will trumpet a balancing act.

Remember, that anger is the fire that cauterizes a wound allowing it to heal. We need other emotions to support and feed the others. I'd promote contentment far before ever promoting happiness alone.

Contentment requires balance; in the midst of a hardship, still recognize the beauty surrounding and you won't drown in the one chaotic event. The extreme opposite of positive psychology is to fixate your focus solely on what is wrong. Consider what is good all while allowing what is hard and hurtful to matter.

This is good. This is balance.

" FORGIVENESS SETS YOU FREE
FROM THE BURDEN OF A
BROKEN HEART, WHETHER YOU
CAUSED THIS BROKENNESS, OR
YOU FEEL BROKEN. "

g u e s t   w r i t e r
MIKE RIZZO
Marriage Counseling Pastor

BE TRUE TO YOURSELF

It's been over four hundred years since Shakespeare wrote the words, "To thine own self be true." A more updated version reads, "Be true to yourself." We all get the gist, right? Being a people pleaser is a barren and tiresome road to travel. I need to be the authentic "me." I heard one Bible teacher sum it up like this: Be yourself. Everybody else is already taken.

Sadly, in this crazy world in which we live, people have missed out on discovering their authentic, inner core. They have been pushed and bullied into becoming what others desire from them. People pleasers by abduction, overpowered as children, enduring the tragedy of being trafficked in their own homes! People-pleasers by spiritual abuse, from "mavericks" operating with no covering, no checks and balances, claiming to represent God, while further inflicting wounds on the soul that's come to them for healing. I rejoice greatly when I see the emergence of precious jewels like Vivia, redeemed, and on a fervent mission of rescue.

To be honest, everyone has a certain measure of living from a false self. Usually, we had to create one in order to survive, or to at least have some control and peace in defining who we are. Suffering the void of healthy love in childhood and teen years, is a rude shove into seeking fulfillment elsewhere. Or worse yet, we can be objectified by others as they pursue their own diabolical self gratification. The girl who cried forgiveness bears the scars of such affliction, but like her Savior, Jesus Christ, those scars are not holding her back from walking in resurrection power. She is putting off the old, and putting on the new.

"Put off your old self which belongs to your former manner of life...Put on the new self, created after the likeness of God in true righteousness and holiness." Eph. 4:22,24 We have "put on the new [spiritual] self who is being continually renewed in true knowledge in the image of Him who created the new self." Col. 3:10 (AMP) The true self emerging requires continual renewal and the old self doesn't always succumb easily. It necessitates our living in a surrendered state.

Think of a sculptor and his unformed piece of stone. You use dynamite, drilling, and hammering to bring a separation and a freedom from the old structure. The stone is free from the mountain but it's not free from itself. Becoming a Christian is like a precious stone being released from a mountain. My eternal destiny is changed in a moment when I'm born again, and then the spiritual formation continues in earnest.

God is the Master Sculptor. My true self emerges, ever increasing, as I'm conformed to the image of Christ. So He chips away everything that isn't Jesus. The false self will never be on display in the finished work. Unlike real stone, we have a voice; the ability to choose for or against the Sculptor's intentions. Something so precious, does not come without a struggle.

In my experience, both personal and in pastoring others, the false self (impostor) is rooted in childhood. Emotional wounding and trauma are a potent force against authenticity. In order for the child to survive, the only option is to become somebody safe. There are at least two sides to this coin, with many variations. Some go inward to build their fortress of safety, while some become aggressive to ensure that they will have control over their life. Because the false self may have been the only friend you had, it can feel unnatural and very confusing, to become someone new, even though you're convinced it's healthy and God inspired. We need trusted allies on the journey.

I love the line in the Crazy World poem, "Stand tall, let your walls fall", to which I would add, in a safe place. Vivia's supporting cast, past and present, share in the trophies of grace that are filling her life. Safe people make for safe healing and recovery. We also need to be kind to our false self as we escort him (her) out the door. It is always a mixture of forgiveness (to our offenders) and repentance (for our reaction to our offenders), and an acceptance of where we are on the ever progressing journey.

We are "fearfully and wonderfully made" - respected by God and distinguished by Him from every other person ever created. Everything good in me, is in the image of God. Thus when I self reflect, my goal is to reflect Christ. "And we all, with unveiled face, continually seeing as in a mirror the glory of the Lord, are progressively being transformed into His image from [one degree of] glory to [even more] glory, which comes from the Lord, [who is] the Spirit. 2 Cor. 3:18 (AMP)

Vivia calls it a "curiosity train." What a great description! A few years ago, when we first met, I could see the pure heart, seeking truth, even though the odds were stacked against her. Her search was, and still is, clothed in mercy, as she seeks to meet everyone at their own unique place in the journey. I have seen the transformation in her heart and life, and a growing wisdom to rest a bit on the glory plateaus until they become a launch pad unto the next level.

A BELOVED PLACE AT THE TABLE

Remember the scene at The Last Supper? The iconic piece of art portrays Christ's inner circle of disciples, responding to the revelation that there was a traitor in their midst. Meal times in the Middle East were akin to our modern day picnic on a blanket. The food was laid on the floor, on a piece of cloth, or perhaps on a slightly raised platform of sorts. There may have been pillows to recline on and you would eat either sitting down or lying on your side. We know from the gospel accounts, that the honored place at the table, reclining next to Jesus, was filled by the Apostle John.

John is known as the "beloved disciple", a description by the way, that is not intended to produce envy or exclusivity in our hearts. Wasn't Jesus close to everyone? Does He not love us all the same? True, but He was mentoring and preparing John to take his place as a literal son, to care for His mother, after His death. Who knows? John's place at the table may have been needful for those specific instructions. There is also the element of receptivity and response. Perhaps John pressed in a bit more to go deep in his relationship with Christ.

When you join the community of disciples, your place at the table is in close proximity to Christ. We all have beloved status. "And He raised us up together with Him and made us sit down together [giving us joint seating with Him] in the heavenly sphere [by virtue of our being] in Christ Jesus (the Messiah, the Anointed One). Eph.2:6 (AMPC) We all have the same relational access. Yet, there is the presence of Judas as well; thus we must be guarded. Overwhelmed by obstacles, Vivia did not give up, even when the counterfeit Christian help showed up, the Judas at the table, if you will. By the grace of God she gained a backbone and learned how to stand up for her true self.

ESCORTS UNTO ENLARGEMENT

Desiring to walk in the "beloved" status for which we are all qualified, will entail the embrace of restraints along the way. Unlikely allies will include: suffering, disciplined yielding, and living the crucified life. Jesus certainly modeled this for us. For John, decades of ministry adventures were his reward, but in his final years he was banished to a Roman penal colony. More than likely, he anticipated his retirement as a Roman prisoner, but God had other plans.

John saw his beloved Jesus on Patmos, but it wasn't the upper room Jesus or the resurrected earthly form of Christ. It was the ascended glorified Christ, overwhelmingly glorious to where John "fell at His feet as though dead." Jesus placed His right hand on John and spoke to him. I wonder if Jesus may have taken at least a moment to embrace His faithful follower? The older I get, the more I understand and appreciate the story-line of my life. The ebbs and flows once deemed narrow and constricting, prove to be escorts unto enlargement. For John, it was writing the Book of Revelation. It behooves us to never call any chapter the final one.

Thank you Vivia, for fighting through your seasons of being banished and exiled by a cruel regime of people. Jesus appears to many in that place, but not all respond to Him. The girl who cried forgiveness, was courageous to embrace the pain of grief. The girl who cried forgiveness was obedient to follow the example of her Jesus, whose final words included a pardon for his killers. Vivia has found her place at the table, and she will not be moved.

What-If City

Changing Your "What if's"!

Many times we use "What if's" in a negative way. For example, people say "what-if's" in a negative way. For example, people say "what if I get fired", "what if my relationship goes bad", and so on and so on. These "what if's" take away our ability to feel joy because they stop us from doing what we really want in life out of fear of "what if".

Try turning your "what if's" into POSITIVE ones! "What if you get a promotion?" and "What if your relationship improves?" Remember, the unconscious mind is powerful and will LOOK FOR whatever you tell it to look for. By saying "What if something amazing happened?" your mind automatically will begin scanning your life for amazing things!

When you pursue this, you are also preparing yourself to find contentment regardless the reality of your outcome. What if everything blows up? What if everything will be ok? Using your imagination, becoming familiar with either situation can prevent anxiety.

The Girl Who Cried Forgiveness

What negative "what if's" do you often think? Rewrite new, positive ones below:

What If...

_____

_____

_____

_____

_____

What If...

_____

_____

_____

_____

_____

What If...

_____

_____

_____

_____

_____

Without Vision

Flower face,
Neck like a vase
Shoulders stronger than before
Won't you pursue the vision?

Pursue the vision or collapse
Sit and wander,
List your "What ifs"
Or take flight
Run after these visions with all your childlike faith
This life is meant to be lived and lively
This life lived on purpose
Your life, on purpose

Every old habit, dark horse
Each scapegoat to keep you on course
We find you running
Far from where you are
So much past inside your present
Afraid of who you truly are
You can't cry, but you're emotional
So far replaced from you who you are to be
Experiencing growth pains
As you prepare to labor
Your truest self
Changing things rather than complaining about them
Confidently supporting people, loving them, preventing the
worst case scenarios
Preventing the dark horse

seventh chapter

24 ON COUNTY 83

Maria and I met when I frequented West Main Street. She'd grown up in the area and with the community. I did not notice her radiant beauty until this community began spitting me out, while Maria welcomed me back with a warm heart and even a home.

I'd found it very challenging to live away from home and attend beauty school. I told her I wanted to quit and she quickly voiced to her Mom that they needed to do something to help me. I did not have the finances for this opportunity nor any financial support. They welcomed me into her home where Maria and I stayed.

Their house was like a cabin and her bedroom was in a loft. In Maria's room there were bunk beds with white sheets detailed with purple, grey and blue flowers on it. She had so many comfy pillows and even some stuffed animals. Justin Bieber posters covered one of her walls at the time and you could tell the main source of entertainment was from the radio on top of her dresser. Finally, I felt at home. Maria loved me so deeply, she fell in love by default.

The Girl Who Cried Forgiveness

I slept on the top bunk the first night, but by the second, we became much closer friends, and I slept every night from then on to Justin Bieber's 13-year-old album, cuddling close to Maria in her bed. This became my constant reminder that everything was going to be okay and that for the time being, we could have fun!

Many days I'd wake up to a terrifying sight. She began playing games with me as she learned my fear for clowns and Gollum from The Lord of the Rings. I was never bored with Maria; there was not a dull Moment I can think of! Most mornings, I'd wake up to her Wocket doll hanging from the bottom of the top bunk, nearly kissing my face! This doll is cute and from Dr. Suess, but when it is a doll that lurks around the home and in a different hiding space each day, it becomes less cute and far more creepy. I learned to walk prepared for this surprise every day! After a Lord of the Rings marathon with friends, Maria decided to freak me out again. This was how we showed love, apparently. My life had been a series of dramatic events so to scare me for fun wasn't very much fun for me, yet I played along. I had just parked Maria's car in her parent's driveway. I began walking down the dirt driveway to the door, talking to Maria, like she was behind me. I looked back for her and saw she was in the car getting her things. She had the key, so I had patience, also a full bladder. Maria saw how I squirmed at each scene featuring Gollum. She found the perfect opportunity to hide in the woods surrounding our home for a couple minutes. Long enough to make me squirm right there at the doorstep. Maria finally came back but running on all fours with her porcelain skin glowing in the night and muttering words Gollum used in the movie, with that creepy imitation of his voice! I screamed! I knew it was her, but the sight was uncomfortable. I was nervous, so I laughed and screamed. She collapsed before reaching me, crying because she was laughing so much.

We had to pipe down so her parents would stay asleep. Poor Terri and Howey had less sleep after I moved in. They were constantly telling us to quiet down as we'd laugh ourselves to sleep and scare each other around every corner in this echoing loft house.

When I was excommunicated from this community, Maria did what she had for anyone else who did not feel welcomed or loved. She maintained a relationship and cried to love as loudly as I cried to forgive. Maria and I carried on our friendship to the point that I called her my best friend. I have so many great memories with her. We would dance, make silly videos, play games, dress up and go out, get into trouble, worship together, and do everything you do with your best girlfriend. I was a bridesmaid in Maria's wedding, where to this very day, she will always stand out in my mind, as the most beautiful bride I have ever seen. Wildflowers in various colors stood all around her, in vases on the ground. At this outdoor wedding she invited everyone she loved, in spite of people's inability to show love to one another.

Maria and her husband had a honeymoon baby. She was so excited about this! Maria's love for kids was so sweet. I could tell she was learning a lot from them. She knew they'd teach her more about hope, faith, fearlessness, and love. Maria was a big kid herself, and so being a Momma was simply a natural thing for her.

I've learned that growing up, Maria had always struggled with a certain level of anxiety. Having experienced the community she grew up in, I can understand feeling the need to please people, and to always appear by the set standards. Her anxiety would sometimes create her aloof, exhausted, (taking many naps daily) and praying constantly against panic.

This made her more susceptible to the baby blues. Maria was soon affected by and diagnosed as Postpartum Depression.

In the US, about 1 in 10 Moms suffer from postpartum depression (PPD). Anyone can be affected regardless of age, number of kids, ethnicity, marital status or income. It can happen to you when you least expect it. The exact cause of this is seemingly unknown. I believe some factors are caused by a family or personal history of depression, increased life stressors, and hormone changes related to pregnancy. Maria was experiencing many life stressors, and her life spent with anxiety did not support her health. Remember in previous chapters that Maria had such a hard time accepting her little family for a while, and the quarrel we had concerning the chosen name for her second baby. Her PPD stuck around after her first baby, and increased postpartum to her second child.

If Postpartum Anxiety persists for more than a couple weeks after birth, it becomes very important to seek help. Maria tried to treat this by carrying on with an active prayer life, and by taking good care of her family. She remained an excellent employee and coworker.

Maria lived in Kansas City for one year as her husband pursued an internship. It was so fun to live so close to her and her new little family! When Maria and I would meet, she'd tell me about her strange nightmares. She told me about them in great detail, as if she could not forget them.

Maria's nightmares involved getting out of bed and throwing her crying baby over the patio, while railing from their second story apartment. Some involved Maria hovering her child over an active burner at the stove. She shared these nightmares with me and we prayed against them, uncertain of what else to do. Maybe it was just a fluke? A bad Pizza Dream? She was a nurse, She was a nurse, after all, and she didn't seem to have any other concerns about this. Maria wasn't one to tell others her problems. She saw herself as the caregiver, and she wanted to help them. I didn't know enough about postpartum depression at this point, to recognize her problem. All I knew was to pray.

One year, Maria celebrated my birthday with me by taking me on a horseback ride with her Aunt Julie; (there was no way this story would be left out of my book) Maria, Julie and I saddled up! As we did, Julie and Maria reminded me of the To-Do's and the Not-To-Do's. At the time of this event, I was wearing a wig for the following reasons: My good friend was killed in an accident by a drunk driver, so another great friend gave me money to get my hair done. Unfortunately, the self-care gift went hay-wire. My hair was dark brown and shoulder length. It was thick, shiny and healthy! I wanted to gradually turn to a blonde color and knew this would be a gradual process. This hairstylist should have taken about a year to execute this vision but rather, the stylist tried to do it in one day. Therefore, my hair color was lifted so much that it wound up falling out. Near my roots, hair strands felt like that of a Barbie doll's hair. If you lit a match, it would have shriveled up to nothing. Soon-after, I had my hair cut into a short pixie cut. I wanted my long hair back so badly, I bought a wig. This wig made me feel less insecure about everything else that had happened.

This wig made me feel less insecure and sad about it. Julie is a hairstylist. Between horseback riding reminders and instructions, she begged me to remove the wig. Julie didn't think it would be that bad, and wanted to assure me that it wasn't. Still insecure, I continued to say no, with a coy posture and tone of voice. I was told not to have my foot too far in the stirrup, for if something happened, then my saddle would not stay secured. Maria knew so much about horseback riding, and was a great support. We went across the road and down a path. Julie shared that she needed to go to the bathroom, so we didn't plan to be out too long. Something stopped us...Maria's horse began to go crazy! He must have smelled the donkey's beyond the bushes! Once Maria's horse became stir-crazy, it became a Domino effect! Maria was yelling for her horse to calm down, cut and suit, and while Julie's horse followed suit, by propping himself up on it's two hind legs. Julie calmly told Maria that yelling would hardly help.

Meanwhile, I'm in my own world on the sidelines. My foot had been too far into the right stirrup, so, naturally, my saddle was now worn on the horse's side, and near to its belly! I was riding sideways on a running horse! I looked ahead and saw a road sign, looked down and saw a heavy hoof. Was I going to be punched unconscious by this horse's wild hoof? Scrape my back on the road sign? Finally, I realized I was closer to the group than I thought, and after releasing my right foot from the tight stirrup, I dropped to the ground, as the horse ran off. Julie jumped off her horse, ran to retrieve mine, while Maria tried to follow Julie's lead, getting off her horse. As I lay in the grass, winded of breath,

I remember looking at the trees touching the sky, thinking, "What just happened?" I was looking around me, while Maria and Julie calmed the horses. Maria was yelling frantically, "I just killed my best friend on her birthday!". Maria ran to me to see if I was alive and well. Julie followed, but not running, more of a waddle, coming my way in very slow motion. As I continued to collect my bearings, I looked up. Behind me, I saw my wig, and my wig cap were now hanging on two separate branches in a tree, with leaves weaved throughout them. This sight made me start to giggle. Then, I noticed Julie's waddle had been to prevent her from chafing, because she had peed her jeans during all the commotion! Julie recognized that I caught her as well, and we both began to laugh very hard. Maria was not amused because she felt more worried and scared, and still holding onto the trauma of the situation.

We then rode our horses back to their stable, laughing all the way. We would tell this story to everyone at home at least three times, before Julie ever changed her jeans. This was such a memorable birthday! This story goes down in history, and is retold every time I visit home.

By the time Maria was expecting her second child, she and her husband decided they needed an army of support at home. They needed more help with babysitting than they could find while living in Kansas City. They moved back to their hometown. Maria started at her new job at a local hospital. Eventually, they left her in-law's resort, to move into her and her husband's first home! Maria was overjoyed!

Being that Maria made my last birthday so special, as well as memorable, we decided she should host this birthday party as well, in her new home. I was on my way to Minnesota. I was not in the best place emotionally, having just broken up with my fiancé, and calling off our wedding, so I needed a safe place to hunker down, a home, I needed Minnesota. While Maria worked, I worked, helping to clean her home. It was always hard for her to keep up. She had to clean after her kids, herself, and her husband. She hardly had any time for herself, between naps, energy supplements, drinks and taking on everyone's unwanted shifts, (even overnight shifts) at work, let alone to keep up with her little family.

I helped to put everything together a bit more before the birthday party. She was very happy to see this!

As my gift, Maria gave me a green book called "About Me: A Memoir". She knew how much I wanted to write this book, so her gift was encouraging and thoughtful. I used the book as a guide while writing this one! She hosted friends of ours that had split up before because of shunning from the community we'd all been a part of. We had great food, fun music, games, and made so many amazing memories!

I spent some time after this, restoring myself emotionally. I thought I needed another break, and so July came, my friend Sarah and I met in-between Kansas City and Oklahoma, for a fun getaway at an Airbnb. When Sarah and I decided in July of 2016 to Marco Polo Maria, (Marco Polo is a video chat on your phone!) we didn't expect her attitude and behavior.

Sarah and I laid in bed resting while messaging Maria back and forth. Maria had been encouraging us to read the Bible more. Some of her comments were very irrelevant to the conversation. Maria seemed more bold than usual, and without a filter. Her usual patience and loving kindness seemed masked by something that had really affected her. We felt she was projecting something onto us. Because this was so out of her character, we decided to let it go.

The Girl Who Cried Forgiveness

Come August, Maria confessed some insecurities about her marriage with me. She felt so distraught. It was starting to become hard to keep up with her. One day, she was crying and talking with me about how to cope. The next day, she was posting videos of herself sharing the gospel with people, and sharing her story to online platforms.

Now, we were trying to encourage one another. These videos had me very concerned. Maria and I had been talking about her receiving counseling offered through work. Her video chats went from extreme highs to extreme lows. She couldn't quite keep up with anything. Come late August, I'd been begging Maria and our friends to help her find peace of mind. I wanted her to come to Kansas City where I could help her. I wanted her to get counseling, use the local prayer room that she loved, and learn how I could support her. I'd babysit for her and clean for her for free. She began to avoid this idea without any reason whatsoever. Her other friends didn't know what to do.

I felt at a loss while in Minnesota visiting my friend Molly. Maria left a frantic voicemail message, where she was crying, and having a panic attack. The plan was for her to come and visit me in Minneapolis. She told me how she was blacking out every twenty minutes, and admitted to me that her family had been having to drive her because of the blackouts. She had to cancel her visit. I carried on with my friends, went to church, and called Maria back. I couldn't stop crying. Maria was experiencing so much pain, without any clarity. I then called her husband from the church lobby, trying to encourage him to bring his family to Kansas City, their safe haven, for a little bit. He could only cry, and cling to a little bit of hope of moving on from this. I travelled back home. I travelled back home to Kansas City. It wasn't too much later I heard from Maria. She was finally getting counseling. She also told me that she thought it best not to talk with me for a while. She said it would be the best for our friendship if we stopped talking for a while. She seemed happy as she said this, while I just couldn't understand. She began telling me everything was going to be okay, and to trust her.

I felt confused. I wondered where Maria was getting her advice. Was she even going to counseling? Could her counselor and co-workers tell something was wrong? Was her husband okay with this? Was everyone only praying or were they acting upon what they were seeing as wrong? By this time, I was at my boiling point. I was livid.

Sarah and I tried to support Maria over our Marco Polo videos by reminding her of her kindness, and that cutting off relationships was against everything she believed in. We reminded her that certain people were vying to get her to cut relationships with others, thus manipulating her, and that wasn't right. Maria had already decided in her heart to cut off certain relationships, including us, and we couldn't talk her out of her decision.

I hadn't talked to Maria for a week-or-so by now. Though she was back in Minnesota and I was still in Kansas City, we usually talked every other day. This felt so strange to me and such a loss because she was my best friend. However, I decided to pray and give her the space she was demanding.

Maria told me she was upset. She thought that I was trying to drive a wedge between her and her husband. She referred to a Marco Polo we sent her husband while Sarah and I were on vacation. In the Marco Polo video, Sarah and I were dressed in thick, extra large, frumpy robes, messaging her husband, so they both might message us back. Maria was notorious for not being near her phone. I usually would call her her husband or Mom to get one of them to tell her to call me back. She took this Marco Polo of Sarah and myself as me driving a seductive wedge between the two of them.

I wanted to defend my case, and more than anything, I wanted to help her. Those videos she shared were driving me crazy, especially, as people made comments to encourage the videos. Many said they were so proud of her and happy for her. While that's not necessarily bad, I was absolutely out of my mind upset that people thought these videos were okay and sane. They weren't! I tried calling Maria and my friends. Neither thought anything major was wrong. They both separately encouraged me to just pray, and reminded me how hard it would be for her to just stop everything, get help, just because I thought she needed it.

September 8, 2016, while out with my friend Will at The Tank Room (a live and local music hub), Maria's brother-in-law called me. I ignored his first call, because I was out. I text him to see what was up. He doesn't usually call me. Usually we would message me with his wife on our thread. He then asked where I was and if I was with someone. I told him I was out with a friend, and asked if it was urgent. I then excused myself out of the building to the sidewalk, and called him. He asked what I was doing. I started telling him all about my night and how great it was, that the music was amazing, and I was finally having some fun since my breakup.

"Maria is dead." he said "She killed herself last night."

I couldn't hold myself together. My throat went dry, my breathing stopped, everything went silent, and my fingers numb. I was in shock, and already diving into absolute outrage. I had to keep it together...I was in public, and downtown at night. I had to go back inside to tell Will that we needed to leave. After talking with her brother-in-law, I escaped to the alley to let out my cry. With knees weak, I fell to the ground. Shaking, I texted Will, told him we needed to leave, that I was just notified that my best friend is dead.

I couldn't feel more grateful to have been with Will that night. I met him through my ex-fiancee. When the breakup happened, he was kind and still a friend. When we left our fun night early, he talked with me to keep my focus on good things, at least until we got home. I fought back the tears to try to keep on a good face. Once I got home, I hurried inside and collapsed.

In the hallway, close to my room, I began to wail, scream, and cry. My roommates ran to embrace me, as I wept.

That night, I didn't sleep. I called a mutual friend of mine, who knew Maria, and told her. I also told my ex-fiancee, as we'd gone on double dates with Maria and her husband. I told my Grandma, who told my Mom. When my Mom heard, she called me right away, breaking our lack of conversation, that had lasted six months or so. I had to call my Grandparents as well. They were headed to Kansas City to begin a new tradition with me, by spending time together on National Grandparent's Day. They were well on their way, and had almost finished the drive. They drove me back home so I could attend Maria's funeral. This trip was immeasurably difficult. My friends, Molly and Marta, came to be with me while a handful of people kept their distance from me, as if I did something wrong. My sister had her baby that morning, with bleeding complications. My Mom was with her, while Grandma Jan wanted to come, but couldn't, as she was sick. I spent time constantly texting my Mom and sister, insisting they learn about Postpartum while in the hospital with professionals.

I felt the most alone I'd ever felt in my life that day. I spent time with Maria's family, in-laws, and other good friends, but couldn't stand being near anyone else. Walking into the wake was the most challenging part for me. How could I do this? This meant Maria was really gone. Seeing her in the casket meant I needed to begin accepting reality.

I am forever grateful for Molly and Marta for spending that time with me. They ate with me, attended the funeral with me, sang with me, and gave me some laughs, while still allowing me to talk and cry about Maria as if she were still with us. I remember many people felt so concerned that this might truly be my last straw. I felt off, I had suicidal ideation, and couldn't stop thinking about Maria. I wasn't thinking of how I could survive this, but how could I have protected her?

There are said to be seven steps of grief. Shock, denial, anger, bargaining, depression, testing and accepting. At this point my shock was dancing with denial. Once I returned home to Kansas City, I dove headfirst into anger and began to bargain or seek a way out of this pain. I began blaming people for not listening to me, imagining the hospital where Maria worked, being on fire, for lack of justice and support they'd shown her. My anger was directed at people, her family, companies myself, and more.

Upon my return, my roommate Rebecca had purchased a spot for me at a weekend intensive in Holden, Missouri. At Harvest Home, people help people. Through prayer and the power of imagination, I was able to begin taking baby steps away from this outrage and bargaining and into the next few stages of grief.

I couldn't sleep. I actually thought up who should have died instead of her. That's awful, and I feel it's a normal response too. After the amazing weekend of driving back and forth to Harvest Homes, a 45 minute drive one way, I joined grief groups. At the time, I was working as a ParaProfessional for Autistic teenagers. If you know anything about autistic behavior, you'd understand that I had gained "autistic accountability" there. I came back from the funeral...different. Less amused, tired, unable to sleep, fighting to smile, without feeling guilty about it. I wore glasses, because maybe that would make me appear less tiresome. I hadn't worn glasses before, so when I chose to, this change was too much for some students. My glasses were broken on my face by the harsh punch of a student.

I listened to John Mayer's song on repeat, "You're Gonna Live Forever in Me," and I meant it. This song and all the shit I'd experienced up to this point in my life, lit me up inside to make it all matter. Maria was not going to just disappear, being someone people would forget about, or fade away into a distant memory. She would live forever. I quickly decided to pursue a Major in Psychology and HR at Avila University. I decided to begin a business supporting Moms by bringing the support they needed; the self-care feeding accountability. I decided to help people now, rather than waiting until my license became active and legal, so I took a test and became a life coach; calling myself a Clarity Coach. It was now time to initiate doing something different, that would bring a life long lasting impact. If I could live a life exhausted and beaten down by people, then I could also live a life excited and passionate by working to protect and restore the hurting ones.

Losing someone you love will never stop hurting. You will never stop missing them. Once you begin to accept they are not here, but in Heaven, living life without them here becomes easier. This pain I felt came in waves, as if you lost your loved one again and again, not just today. it keeps coming and going in waves. Certain things trigger fond memories while other triggers are painful. Expect this when you're grieving.

Imagine you're at the beach watching the waves. Some waves rush in to sweep over your feet while others thrash up against your body hard enough to knock you down. These big waves sound like thunder. The sound ricochets across your memories taking you deeper into grief. The loss never goes away but the grief lessens just as the ocean will also come to a calm.

Group therapy helped me by proving to me that I wasn't alone. It also encouraged me to do something about this pain, to let the loss matter. I saw people who'd been attending this group for years. I didn't last more than one month, because I couldn't sit in that grief, in that competition of who's loss outweighed the other's more.

When you're stuck in What-If City, answer your questions, no matter how painful your answers.

What if I could have saved Maria? What if I could have done more or told her parents instead of our friends? What if I didn't allow her to push me away? What if? What if? What if? Resolve this pain by answering your own questions. If you could have, would you have? If you would have known, would you have helped? Now plan, so you can support someone else struggling with this, because Maria wasn't alone even if she thought she was. There was help without a plan and she needed both.

g u e s t   w r i t e r
MARY POPE
CEO, Oh Baby! KC

It was a beautiful day in May 2019, Vivia and I had been Instagram friends for a short time, and had not yet met in person. We were both set up as vendors at a local mom-centered event with one booth between us. We met briefly in the midst of the busy-ness of speaking to moms and other business owners. During that brief, yet meaningful conversation, Vivia and I had a deep connection that happens between people with similar visions and purposes.

Our words resonated with each other and we became fast friends. Our goals of supporting moms who are struggling, need community and to feel like their best selves again, mirrored each other although our businesses were different, and we have since discovered that in supporting each other as colleagues and friends, we can better serve the women who lean on us for support. I am honored to have this opportunity to contribute to Vivia's writing and to offer a small portion of what I do to help families thrive.

Postpartum mental health disorders can be so tricky to spot! There is a lot going on that makes recognizing a mood disorder difficult. Lack of sleep, change in routine, and thinking that "this is how it's supposed to be", can all contribute to not seeing that you are, in fact, struggling. The postpartum period is a life-changing and very vulnerable time. So often, parents focus on preparing for the birth of their baby - as they should! - but very little time is spent on preparing for postpartum. A large part of this, may be because so many women are silent about it, struggle through it and believe that this is the only way.

I've been married to a disabled army veteran for nearly a decade. Noticing mental health struggles is simply a part of life around here. There are things that we do in our home, and with our family, that most people do not, or have never had to think about! When I became a doula and started working with parents through their pregnancies, postpartum and even in loss, I started to see how the tools I have as a wife of a veteran, was an invaluable resource to the families I serve. In the next few pages, I want to give you some very practical tools and knowledge that will prepare you for what is normal and that could be your lifeline if needed.

First of all, let's do some postpartum mental health myth busting! I'm going to list the myths we tell ourselves (and society has told us) about perinatal mood disorders (PMAD) and switch those up with the truth.

Myth: Having a PMAD means I am a bad mother!

Truth: Having a PMAD does not make you a bad parent any more than having a physical illness does. If you caught the flu, nobody would tell you that you're a bad parent. Someone might just bring you soup!

Myth: I am not feeling sad or weepy, so what I'm struggling with must not be postpartum depression.

Truth: Perinatal mood disorders are not limited to depression. If you are experiencing anxiety, intrusive thoughts, OCD, panic or post traumatic stress, those are all valid struggles with a PMAD.

Myth: PMADs and "the baby blues" are the same thing.

Truth: They are not. The baby blues happen with 80% of women, tend to only last a little while, go away on their own and are primarily "just" being weepy or emotional. PMADs are intense hormone fluctuations, and do not resolve on their own, can last for years if left untreated, can affect your sleep and your appetite, can make you feel detached from your baby and make you feel isolated.

Myth: If I seek help for a PMAD, my baby will be taken away from me.

Truth: Having a mental health disorder or seeking help is not a criminal act and the people who are able to help want to see you and your family thrive together!

Myth: I have a PMAD because I am weak.

Truth: PMADs are chemical/hormonal imbalances. Being pregnant, giving birth and then regulating afterward requires an incredible amount of hormones shifting and changing - none of this is your fault nor does it mean you are weak.

Myth: Nobody will understand if I tell them that I am not bonding with my baby, think about harming my baby, or think of harming myself.

Truth: There are many people who will not only understand, but be able to help you and give you a light at the end of the tunnel completely judgment free!

Myth: I will be judged harshly if I have to take medication or see a therapist.

Truth: Medication and therapy are powerful and useful tools available to us. Again, nobody judges people who have to take medication for a physical illness or for going to physical therapy after an accident - you will not be judged for taking medication or going to therapy either.

Myth: PMADs only happen within the first 12 weeks postpartum.

Truth: PMADs can show up anytime in the first year.

Some women notice it prominently after they wean.

You probably have an emergency plan or fire escape route for your family. Having this doesn't mean that your home will catch on fire, but it simply means that in the case of an emergency you are prepared, can stay calm, remain objective and all of your family members are likely to escape safely.

Your fire escape route probably includes your front door or your back door. You use these all the time, not only during a fire. But if those options were cut off from you, you and your family would know which windows are their best options to reach safety.

Think of your postpartum plan like a fire escape route. Just like you use your doors daily, your plan can be used in the best of circumstances. It can be used when your baby is sleeping well, breastfeeding is going exactly according to plan, your hormones are balancing out in a timely manner and it all seems pretty steady and sweet. But the plan also transforms into an emergency escape when you feel like you are trapped, scared and without options. Knowing what to watch for, having a plan for care, being informed on what is not normal and knowing who to turn to for help may literally save your life.

Creating a plan is simply making note of what your life before having your baby looks like and assuming that you'll either need to compensate for each area, let some things go for a little while or delegate help. Let's break these down together!

What are some things that you do everyday or every week without fail? Things that are necessary to a good quality of life.

- Prepare and eat food,
- Shower,
- Sleep,
- Go to the grocery store,
- Go to the gym,
- Clean your home (dishes, laundry, sweep/wash floors)
- Anything else you would add?

Now take those basic life needs and assume that you are going to need help with all of them. This is about setting realistic expectations and making your life as a new parent easier!

Delegate as much as possible. I realize that not everybody can hire help, but I want to mention what is out there, because I also don't want to assume that nobody can hire help.

- Postpartum Doula
- Meal Prep and/or Grocery Delivery
- House cleaning

Having your basic needs cared for takes the guesswork out of your mental health. Are you struggling with depression or have you simply not slept in 4 days? Is what you are feeling postpartum rage or are you hangry? Do you have postpartum anxiety or do you feel like you have no solid routine in place? I am not saying that these things will "cure" perinatal mood disorders, but they do help to remove the blurred lines so that help can be sought sooner.

Let's talk about creating a support network now. These may be things you've never had to utilize before and may not realize you may need until, well, you do! So let's not reinvent the wheel and let me help you take the guesswork out of it. I recommend getting these in place during your pregnancy. Have things set up, find out which of these services are in your area, make contact with the professionals, and interview them if possible. Find people you resonate with and can trust. If you do not have them in your area, contact some that offer remote services.

1. Therapist who specializes in Perinatal Mood Disorders and birth trauma.
2. IBCLC, lactation counsellor or a La Leche League - when breastfeeding is not going smoothly, you want to have already made a connection and have contact information.
3. Contact a sleep specialist or counselor for a consultation. Knowing how to establish a good sleep schedule and routine for your baby from day one will help you feel more in control of your circumstances. I am NOT suggesting that you sleep train your newborn! What I am recommending is knowing how to establish good sleep habits and to be proactive.
4. Find a local moms group that does meetups and can be a support network and encouragement source.
5. Put the number for Postpartum Support International in your and your partner's phones: 1(800)944-4773, #1 for Spanish #2 for English. This is not an Emergency number, but rather a good resource for if you are struggling and need a listening ear.
6. Have the phone number for the National Suicide Prevention Hotline (1-800-273-TALK (8255)) somewhere easy to find. Put it in your phone or have it on your fridge door. Again, this is your fire escape plan. You hope you never have to use it, but if you do, you'll be glad it was literally at your fingertips!

There is so much more we could say on this topic, but

that is the basics of creating a postpartum support plan. We have noted what your normal looks like, how to seek assistance to maintain your normal as closely as possible, and have established a safety net that will catch you if you need it to. A fire escape plan that you hope you don't have to use, but man, if you need it, no time is wasted and you can get the help you need fast!

"GRIEF DOES
NOT HAVE A
TIMEFRAME.
IT BUILDS AND
CALMS IN WAVES."

The Girl Who Cried Forgiveness

After losing Maria post-wedding chaos, I felt exhausted. This was the last straw and I wasn't convinced I could hold myself back from following suit to a death by suicide. I had to act quickly. I was self-aware. Aware of the ticking time bomb I became and just what my vices were. When I wanted to be alone, I made myself leave that time alone to be with people in grief groups and with my friends or at a public 24/7 prayer room. Having others to focus on while swallowed by my self-pity and anxiety, helped me.

There are seven steps of grief. My grief processed through each of the 7 and in an order perhaps unconventional. That was okay and better for me. It is important to know that your healing could look so different from they way others heal and process through grief. It could take longer or shorter. It could become easier quicker than for others. Nothing is wrong with this, it is simply something that is unique about you.

I went to grief counseling. I prayed. I went to an intensive weekend get-away as to assure myself safe and seen. In the quiet, I let this pain breathe. I allowed it to matter. From there on, I had to share more about this person I loved and lost. It was rather complicated and my heart literally heart. Her heart was the one compromised by a knife and it was as if I could feel that stab in my own heart.

The thing to truly bring restoration from such awful memories was in fact, EMDR sessions.

7 Steps of Grief

S h o c k
Initial paralysis at hearing bad news.

D e n i a l
Trying to avoid the inevitable.

A n g e r
Frustrated outpouring of bottled-up emotion.

B a r g a i n i n g
Seeking in vain for a way out

T e s t i n g
Seeking realistic solutions

A c c e p t a n c e
Finally finding a way forward

These "steps" are normal. Everything you've felt from learning of the bad news to now is normal.

I've tried avoiding normalcy in my vernacular while grieving because my relationship and my loss was so much greater than anyone else could imagine. Truthfully, I have never been alone in this seemingly competitive thought, though my paralysis and frustration would deny it.

Have you ever lost someone and the first question from others has been, "How close were you two?" Those grieving this loss alongside you seem to consider who was truly closest rather than grieving together. This can cause mutual friends to the lost ones to separate. Being together without this person is challenging because then their loss is emphasized even more.

My Shock

When Maria passed I was stunned. This seemed more difficult to grasp as a new reality while in another state. I was in Kansas while Maria was in Minnesota. Until I was at her funeral, I couldn't believe what I'd heard was true. I collapsed and felt numb. How could such a powerful presence in my life have left in a moment? Gone.

My Denial

I knew doing this would not help,

Seventh Chapter

What if you could forgive everyone who's ever wronged you? Would you do it? What if forgiving others for offending you would set you up for success, freedom, and the ability to empathize and support others better? Would you commit to such a process as forgiveness? Would you forgive yourself, if you knew it would restore confidence and instill humility? Would you forgive yourself if it removed a victim mentality? What if forgiveness is more for you, than for those who've hurt you?

I cried forgiveness after each crashing wave and I will cry forgiveness for the rest of my days.

FIN.

OTHER RESOURCES
& WORKSHEETS

The following worksheets *do not take place of* therapy, but are intended to *work in partnership* with therapy.

Use this section as a journal, unapologetically responding to each page. If the question provokes anger, let it matter, and write out that anger. If the question provokes sadness, let it matter, and write out that sadness.

These worksheets are a great resource to use in the gap between counseling appointments. Utilize this book as a supporting tool to improve your self-esteem and learn to cope well.

Mindset

By the root of yourself comes the private and most valuable thing creating you able to succeed in life; this is your ability to believe in yourself and what you are capable of doing.

Not only is your growth mindset something powerful, but just as well, having something else to believe in. Something to give yourself to that supports you while removing burdens from your shoulders that you are not meant to carry; making boundaries easier to lay down and live by to protect yourself and others.

There is power in belief. Regardless to what you believe in spiritually or religiously, this mindset leads to amazing opportunities. Those with a growth mindset are able to increase the probability of success more-so than not and overtime.
  If we are to build our potential, we must think differently so that we might perform differently. You can build your abilities bringing your game to new levels.

There are physiological manifestations to mindset. For people with a "fixed mindset", the brain becomes most active when they learn how they performed (a good score or how they are judged). For people with a "growth mindset" the brain becomes most active when they receive information on what they could do better next time (learning how to improve).

As I consider limiting beliefs and the worksheet within this book, I consider culture and how subcultures can feed my fixed belief system. I am not a fan of this. The fixed mindset suggests to me that God is one way and that way is black and white. My growth mindset suggests that God is so big that he truly does love unconditionally, in every community, regardless to your state of mind and stature, God loves relentlessly and unconditionally.

Having faith, having an open and growth mindset prepares you for your most success without the burdens or limitations by popularity or judgement.

New Habit: Mindset

KNOW THE DIFFERENCE

What do you believe in? What do you believe in because that is what you were taught? What do you believe in because that is the popular thought? Know the difference and find contentment and confidence in knowing what you believe in and against regardless of those around you.

FIND CONTENTMENT IN CHANGE

Two things are inevitable in life. That is death and change. These two things will always happen throughout time in every one person's life. When you find yourself with a fixed mindset now, give yourself the permission to change your mind as you please. This is the growth mindset invitation.

MAKE TIME FOR YOURSELF

Often, it is more challenging to develop your own world view and belief system when/if you are always surrounded by the same people with the same ideas. Branch out! Take time for yourself, go somewhere new and experience new mindsets so that you may never feel stuck and you may always return to what you, yourself, believes about the world and your purpose in it.

Negative and Positive Connotations

Negative Cognitions	Positive Cognitions
Self-Defectiveness	
I am not good enough	I am good enough
I am a bad person	I am a good person
I don't deserve love	I deserve love
I am not lovable	I am lovable
I am inadequate	I am adequate
I am worthless	I have velue
I am weak	I am strong
I am permanently damaged	I am healthy (or can be)
I am shameful	I have value
Responsibility	
I should have done something	I did the best I could
I should have known better	I do the best I can
I should have done more	I did my best
I did something wrong	I learned from my mistakes
It's my fault	It's okay to make some mistakes
Safety/Vulnerability	
I am not safe	I am safe now
I can't trust anyone	I can choose who to trust
I am in danger	It's over, I am safe now
I can't protect myself	I can (learn to) take care of myself
I am going to die	I am alive right now
It's not okay to show my emotions	I can safely feel & show emotions
Control/Choice	
I am not in control	I am in control now
I am powerless	I have choices now
I am helpless	I control my destiny
I am weak	I am strong
I cannot be trusteed	I can be trusted
I canot trust myself	I can (learn to) trust myself

Unhealthy Thought Patterns

ALL-OR-NOTHING THINKING

Also known as black or white thinking, this thought pattern is grounded in extremes One misstep on a diet is grounds for complete abandonment of a healthy lifestyle. Falling short of perfection translates into complete failure. Common vocabulary includes words such as never, always and forever instead of more accurate and realistic descriptions.

OVERGENERALIZATION

One unwanted event or experience leads to the general conclusion that nothing ever goes right. A low grade in schools, a rejection from a low interest or criticism at work can be generalized into feelings of defeat and failure. Since all other cases will be the same, you lose the motivation to take risks and keep trying.

MENTAL FILTER

Everything goes right but one little detail was off. Rather than feeling good and focusing on the positive, you dwell on the one negative detail. You don't choose what happens to you, but you can choose how you respond. If you filter out all of the positives, you will miss out on all of the great things life has to offer.

DISQUALIFYING THE POSITIVE

By disqualifying the positive, you turn the best things in life into a negative. A good job is never good enough. Even if you achieve your goals, you minimize your accomplishments and believe anyone could've done what you did. A common example is assuming someone compliments you only because they want something.

JUMPING TO CONCLUSIONS

Even in the absence of facts, you have a negative interpretation. For example, you arbitrarily conclude that someone dislikes you despite a

Unhealthy Thought Patterns

lack of evidence. Or perhaps you assume that something will go wrong - you'll fail the test or get passed over for a promotion - to protect yourself from possible disappointment. In most cases, these worries and fears are wholly unfounded and never come to fruition.

MAGNIFICATION & MINIMIZATION

In addition to minimizing your positive traits, you exaggerate your shortcomings or problems. Focusing on the bigger pictures will help keep the minor mistakes and problems in perspective.

EMOTIONAL REASONING

Feelings are treated like facts in your mind, rather than subjective perceptions that change over time. For example, feelings of guilt mean you're a terrible person and being afraid of something means you're in real danger.

SHOULD STATEMENTS

You feel disappointed, guilty, frustrated or angry when things don't go the way you had hoped or expected. Self-talk commonly includes words such as should, must, have to and ought to. In addition to having unrealistic expectations for yourself, you demand a lot from others and get upset when they fall short. Should statements can be combated by working on the things you can change and accepting the rest.

LABELING & MISLABELING

Labeling relies on the premise that you are what you do. Rather than describing specific actions and behaviors, you give yourself (and others) a label. For example, making a mistake earns you the label of "loser" or "failure" in your own mind. Labels are abstractions that serve little purpose other than to frustrate and lower self esteem. Sometimes they

Unhealthy Thought Patterns

become self-fulfilling prophecies. When directed at others, labels allow youtube brand people as "bad" rather than recognizing a problem with their thinking or behavior (or your own).

PERSONALIZATION

An event that isn't entirely within your control becomes your fault because you hold yourself personally responsible. If a child gets a poor grade in school, the mother may tell herself that this shows what a bad mom she is instead of helping her child. Personalization commonly leads to feelings of shame, inadequacy and guilt. Some people go to the other extreme, blaming others for their problems rather than accepting their role.

Rational Thought Replacement

1. Identify a self-statement that is negative and inaccurate.

___

2. Thoughts and feelings related to the statement.

___

3. Rate the extent (1-10) to which you believed the statement when you were thinking it.

___

4. What actual evidence is there for this idea?

___

5. What evidence exishsts that this idea is false?

___

6. What is the worst thing that could happen to me?

___

7. What can I say to myself to help me reduce false thinking?

___

8. Rate your belief (1-10) in your rational response.

___

9: Re-rate your belief (1-10) in your negative self-talk.

___

10. Specify the emotions associated with that self-talk exercise.

___

Cognitive Behavior Thought Log

Date:

Situation:	Automatic Thought:	Feeling:

Behavior:	Rational Thought:

Date:

Situation:	Automatic Thought:	Feeling:

Behavior:	Rational Thought:

Date:

Situation:	Automatic Thought:	Feeling:

Behavior:	Rational Thought:

Gratitude

Things I'm greatful for:

_____

_____

_____

_____

People I love:

_____

_____

_____

_____

Things I'm good at:

_____

_____

_____

_____

Fun memories:

_____

_____

_____

_____

_____

Sleep

When we sleep, our brain does not shut down. During REM sleep, our brain is just as active as when we are awake. While we sleep, our memories formed that day and strengthens the important ones in a process called "consolidation."

The brain does this by replaying memories. When a new memory is formed, your nuerons fire in a specifc pattern and while you sleep, your brain replays those patterns. If you can remember a gift you got from your fourth birthday, thank the restful nights that followed.

Not getting enough quality sleep can impair your memory and concentration. It can make you feel sluggish. Even lesser amounts of quality sleep can make you more angry and stressed out. That is because poor sleep impairs communication between the part of the brain that deals with planning and self-control. Those brain regions works together to keep your emotions in check; when they are out of sorts, so are you.

Sleep deprivation is also a common symptom of anxiety, depression and bipolar disorder. A lack of sleep might contribute to mental health disorders.

Some people have blamed cheese for causing nightmares. Apparently, different cheeses produced different types of dreams. Really, I think this is a placebo effect by those who've heard of cheese or pizza dreams already. If you are having night terrors, truly awful nightmares, seek Cognitive Behavioral Therapist or an EMDR therapist for more support.

Sleep is so important! When it is challenging to get it, know that sleeping pills do not really help you sleep, they sedate you but do not help you totally sleep and prompt more health risks. They may cause memory damage overtime due to not having the necessary process mentioned before. Consider not numbing your lack of quality sleep and treat the issues truly. Again, I consider EMDR and CBT great theraputic remedies for this concern.

New Habit: Sleep

FALL ASLEEP TO NATURE SOUNDS OR WHITE NOISE

I use an app that plays rain sounds for the elotted time selected. After my usual 9-9.5 hours , the rain fades away and I wake up by the absence of this sound.

WARM TEA BEFORE BED

Chamomile is popular for its calming effect. This herb is best used when you might feel unable to sleep and/or overly stressed.

NATURAL SLEEP AIDS

Natural sleep aids will help to calm your body and mind enough to find good sleep. Vitamins, minerals and healthy herbs are wonderful to support this! It helps you to prepare for a restful and normal sleep cycle without sedatives. That numbing sedation will not restore your energy nor enhance your mental and physical activity for the day to follow. Try

Try melatonin, chamomile and stimulus control, cognitive therapy and relaxation techniques such as meditation and breathing exercises.

The Girl Who Cried Forgiveness

Sleep Diary

Complete in the morning	M	T	W	TH	F	SA	SU
I went to bed at this time:							
I got up this morning at:							
I slept for a total of this many hours:							
I woke up during the night this many times:							

Complete in the evening	M	T	W	TH	F	SA	SU
# of caffeinated drinks today:							
Time of last caffeinated drink:							
Minutes of exercise completed today:							
What I did in the hour before I fell asleep:							
Mood today: (1 = awful, 10= great)							

Nature

I spend most of my spare time writing and listening to instrumental music or bird sounds. As someone who lives with anxiety, these sounds offer quite the peace of mind. I know that I need more support when even this ounce of silence is too loud and impairing my ability to sit still in the sounds of rushing water or the acoustic guitar.

Think about it...every city and town offers parks. They may be small, still they are very beautiful. Parks do not generate income but they do offer a respite from city life keeping us grounded; they are very much valuable to and for a community.

People travel to the middle of nowhere to be surrounded by trees, we camp and hike and we even maintain gardens at our homes. When you feel stressed, do you go for walks outside? Would you rather be seated by a wall or a window with a view? Hospital patients with a view recover faster. Note that when seeking an apartment, we always hope for a balcony at least. As human beings, we clearly crave nature.

Nature is good for your mental health. Doing outdoor activities is positively associated with higher life satisfaction! People feel more energectic when in or even considering nature. Natural scenery generally improves a person's state of mind. They may feel happier and less upset.

Our desire and need for nature is engrained within us to be attracted to nature as our ancestors began there with just that. Some research shows that short term exposure to nature can improve our mood, lower our heart rate, reducing chortesol levels and better immune functioning. Directed Attention Fatigue: when we are highly distracted by outdoor care alarms, phones ringing, and all the barauge of sights, sounds and smells, the more stressed and irritable we might become. In nature, we do not need to spend so much energy in all the distractions but we feel calm, cool and collected.

New Habit: Nature

TAKE A WALK

When I feel I've hit a wall during writing, I know it's time to walk down the road so I might hit 'refresh'! Walking alone with stimulus control clears my mind enough to be able to dive back into work.

When I feel stressed during a conversation with someone, I take a walk. Walking side-by-side while trying for conflict resolution relieves pressure from the situation.

SIT BY THE WINDOW

You may feel stuck when within a building meant to do work. At the very least, relocate near a window or with a view before you. If you cannot stay in that area, take breaks to step outside and enjoy the view! You might even consider decorating your workspace with nature photos.

TAKE SOME TIME OFF

 Have something to look forward to and unplug! When you are able to vacate, develop boundaries and set your intetion for the trip. Know that you may change your mind if you wish to.

List of Fun Activities

PLACES TO GO

park
coffee shop
ice cream parlor
museum
zoo
gym
pool
farmers market
library
mall
movie theater
bowling alley
craft store
garage sale
open house
theme park
comedy club
piano bar

CHORES

clean your car
clean out fridge/freezer
organize a room
check the mail
oragnize your garage
make a budget
groom your dog
make a meal plan
make appointments
mow the lawn

OUTDOOR

go for a walk
ride a bike
swim laps
play a sport
go fishing
fly a kite
watch the sunset
build a bonfire
go kyaking
nap in a hammock
go hiking
take a drive
swing at the park
rollerblade
ride a horse
run a 5k

HOBBIES

learn an instrument
knit/crochet
plant a garden
organize photos
browse Pinterest
cook something
dance class
take a free online class
jigsaw puzzle
read a book
start a scrapbook
write a song

List of Fun Activities

SERVE OTHERS
volunteer at a soup kitchen
bake cookies for local police
visit nursing home
buy a meal for someone
donate clothes
volunteer to babysit
mow someone's lawn
wash someone's car
write thank you notes
volunteer at pet shelter

SELF CARE
take a bubble bath
paint your nails
go shopping
go to a spa
get a facial
get a massage
make your own facial
shave your legs
light a candle
listen to classical music
play with your hair
take a yoga class
get your hair cut

GROUP ACTIVITIES
play board gmes
play cards
take a road trip
go bowling
go dancing
ultimate frisbee
hang at the lake
start a book club
disk golf
game night
go out to eat
explore the city

FOOD
eat a bowl of ice cream
bake a pie
cook your favorite meal
have a picnic
drink a soda
get a milkshake
order a pizza
plan a dinner party
have some herbal tea
go to your fave restaurant
get Chinese takeout
make a smoothie

List of Fun Activities

M I S C
Netflix binge
text a friend
play video games
look through old photos
go window shopping
play with your pet
try online dating
write a letter to a relative
rearrange your furniture
browse the web
play solitaire
attenda a play/musical
attend a concert
plan a vacation
take a day trip
dye your hair
plan your week
make life goals
take a nap
go to bed early
have a glass of wine
buy Christmas gifts
buy a hamster
shop online
write yelp reviews
read a magaine
watch Youtube videos
listen to the radio
start a part time job
open an Etsy store
sell stuff on Craigslist

sing loudly
draw a picture
write a poem
start a blog
call a family member

Fun Activity Log

Date:

What did you do?	How did you feel?	What did you think?

Date:

What did you do?	How did you feel?	What did you think?

Date:

What did you do?	How did you feel?	What did you think?

Date:

What did you do?	How did you feel?	What did you think?

Exercise

Regular aerobic exercise can improve cognitive function and slow cognitive decline. To promote your long-term memory as you age, consider a fitness plan now! Not only will your muscles grow stronger but so will you brain.

Your brain can become protected from depression, altzhiermers disease or dimensia. Physical activity, simply moving your body, can improve your brain and last the rest of your life.

There are brain changing effects of exercise. After each sweat inducing workout you might try, you may feel stronger, lose weight you wish to and because with exercise your long term memory and strengthen your ability to focus and maintain attention for longer periods of time.

Exercise is perhaps the most transformative thing you can do for your brain today because a single workout you do will immediately shift your mood, energy and attention for the better with a long lasting effect.

It can improve your ability to shift and maintain attention. A single workout will improve your reaction times too!

Change your exercise regime to get the long lasting affects so that your brain's anatomy may change for the better.

The more you're working out, the bigger and stronger your hyppacamups and prefrontal cortex become supportive against cognitive decline! This makes it take longer for diseases to take affect.

You simply want 3-4 times a week minimum, 30 minutes an excersie getting your heart rate up! Walk around the block, take stairs, do yoga and grow your brain for long lasting positive and healthy cognitive growth!

New Habit: Exercise

LIVE SIMPLY

I have told people that lifting babies as a nanny through college was it for me. Truly, that was a lot. Babies grow heavier and toddlers want to jump on want to do so much!

PLAY WITH KIDS

Kids will absolutely support this notion! Not only is childlikeness supportive of your ability to hope and use your imagination without fear, spending time with toddlers also will increase your cardio =o workout regime, absolutely! Jump on the trampoline, have a dance party, play kickball, walk to the park! Do what the kids want to do with them!

TAKE THE STAIRS

Not only will I choose to staircase over the elevator but I'll also park further away from the enterance of theg rocery store or coffee shop. Take that extra step!

YOGA

Yoga has been very powerful for my core and cognitive fitness. It's also tought me how to focus on one thing at a time and how to maintain being intentional. There are now free to cheap classes everywhere! Get your stretch on and free your mind!

Daily Food Intake

Breakfast

_____

_____

Lunch

_____

_____

Dinner

_____

_____

Snacks   Drinks

_____   _____

_____   _____

_____   _____

In your opinion, did you eat healthy today?

_____

_____

How was your overall mood today?

_____

_____

_____

Money

As I write this page now, I can relate with you who have been experiencing money problems AND mental illness. If you're waking up in the morning with a black cloud over your head or have early morning anxiety, your finances will go down the tube because you can't move.

Anxiety makes money problems worse and money problems make anxiety worse.

I encourage you to seek a way outside of reliance on medications to bring you peace. In August of 2019, I took a Xanax 2-3 times a day that entire month. I then began decreasing my intake, knowing I did not want to risk addiction. This prescription became when I lost a job unexpectedly as the couple I'd nannied for were finalizing their divorce. Even today, January 2020, I write this after beginning my day with morning anxiety and this fight to keep my breathing under control while holding my tears back.

Money problems lower your self-esteem. Lack of money increases isolation because it makes social connection outside of work more difficult. When people want to go out to dinner or to see a movie and you cannot even spend money on something as small, you might just avoid it. Maybe your ESA is sick and you must choose to spend the money to save the pet or not. The very thing you need to treat your anxiety and depression might cost you, such as community or pets or the ability to work. When you're not working and you don't have health insurance, how can you receive support? Therapy sessions? Medication? As you do this, you might find more peace then financial freedom. It's being able to do it that is the tricky part. There are many ways and I am committed to being one of your avenues. Ask your local support systems how they can work with you.

Those emotionally strained by their financial struggles become more hostile, irritable or uncommunicative toward their loved ones. Rich people can also experience less satisfaction in their lives and relationships due to working so much. Wether you have money or you don't, you will only have strong relationships if you share experiences, add value to friend's lives, keep your promises, have open communication and be on the same page when it comes to financial matters.

DOES MONEY MAKE PEOPLE CONFIDENT?

Money has nothing to do with confidence. What is your state of mind? In some cultures, being tall is considered better than being short and so being that short person or someone married to a short person, you may feel less confident. A majority of people believe money makes a person feel more confident and worthy, but truly, it doesn't. What you might do with the money impacts your confidence more-so. Materialistic things age out of style and user-ability. Many experience stress from buyer's remorse because they are easily interchangeable with other objects. You get a new car but there's a newer model out in six months.

How we allocate our money leads us into confidence and more lasting happiness than things can. Happiness can instill confidence by using money to get life experiences with people and developing good memories. Only spending time and money on these types of experiences can truly instill confidence within you. That's not to say you need a big trip elsewhere, but at to weigh in on experiences over materialistic cravings.

So if you are one struggling with mental illness and money problems, know that money will not make you happier. If it pays your rent and feeds you, find gratitude. If it does not, find support for your mental health so that you are able to and grow in contentment and gratitude still.

There is help.
You are not alone.
This too shall pass.

New Habit: Money

KNOW YOUR PRIORITIES OUTSIDE OF THE SOCIETY'S

What is important to you? Outside of the cookie cutter worlds, what do you wish for? Is it the tiny home? Is it a large home? Is it to travel more or to be able to leave much money behind for your children? Is it to give more? Discover this, aim toward your goal and pace yourself as you grow in this.

GRATITUDE & CONTENTMENT

What do you have? What things do you already own that you are grateful for? Shelter, food, showering. Remember those things are not things everyone have access to. Most often, people are extreme. Either extremely sad or extremely happy; find the balance in being content in the little things and hard times. This will shift how you respond to life when things don't go as planned or take you by surprise.

IF YOU CAN'T, ASK FOR HELP!

If you can't do it, ask for help. If you can however it stresses you out so much, ask for help. You do not have to do this alone. Find out what you get to do to grow your income and your ability to pay your rent and for food. Consider places you might volunteer so that you feel that you can contribute to society even with limited finances.

Symptoms of Stress

rate from 1-10	M	T	W	TH	F	SA	SU
Hostility							
Irritability							
Phobias							
Obsessions							
Headaches							
Backaches							
Irritable bowel							
Constipation							
Muscle spasms							
Insomnia							
Depression							
Withdrawls							
Anger							
Resentment							
Fears							
Neck Aches							
Indigestion							
Ulcers							
Diarrhea							
Nervious tics							
Physica weakness							
Low self-esteme							

Clarifying Values

Check the appropriate box after each statement based on what you value.

	not important	somewhat important	very important	value
Beauty & Aesthetics				
Change & Variation				
Community Life & Citizenship				
Creativity				
Education & Learning				
Family				
Financial Freedom				
Friends & Social Life				
Fun & Enjoyment				
Honesty & Integrity				
Humor				
Intimate Relationships				
Parenting				
Physical Self-Care & Health				
Power & Authority				
Recreation & Leisure				
Sexuality				
Spirituality				
Work & Career				

Support Team

Terapist: Contact:

_____   _____

Psychiatrist: Contact:

_____   _____

Dietician: Contact:

_____   _____

Mentor: Contact:

_____   _____

Accountability: Contact:

_____   _____

Support Friend: Contact:

_____   _____

Other: Contact:

_____   _____

Other: Contact:

_____   _____

Other: Contact:

_____   _____

Emotional Support Animals

Emotional support animals are wonderful. I have a cat named Lady, and a dog named Yogi. These two have made me feel peace during stressful times, and calmed severe panic attacks by their presence alone. Have you ever needed support, wanted it from someone close to you, but didn't care to hear what they had to say? Sometimes, what people say is not helpful but a trigger to an additional mental bomb. ESA's offer support, not a fix, but support.

After an unexpected financial crisis, I found grave concern about my ability to breathe at all. I had panic attacks daily, and they triggered past traumas. I tried natural remedies before deciding to take Xanax until my EMDR therapies removed the weight of the world from my shoulders. I knew I needed more support during my transition, and I didn't want more psychotherapy (talk therapy), so, my EMDR Therapist wrote me an ESA Letter waving the pet fee at the apartment complex I lived in, and then I found Lady.

We should never fully rely on one form of support. There is not one thing to ever cure all anxiety, fear, or trauma. We must do what we can to find a collaborative support system, for me that was EMDR sessions, an emotional support animal, my encouraging friends, my faith in God, and the financial help I received from my boss and family. Do you feel a support animal would help you? Talk with your therapist to move forward.

While many support systems help us, they do not cure us. I encourage you to remember your ability to cope aside your new furry friend, while still pursuing your people relationships and finding satisfaction with them, too.

List of Coping Thoughts

"This situation won't last forever"

"I've already been through so many other painful experiences, and I've survived."

"This too shall pass"

"My feelings make me uncomfortable right now, but I can accept them."

"I can be anxious and still deal with the situation."

"I'm strong enough to handle what's happening to me right now."

"This is an opportunity for me to learn how to cope with my fears."

"I can ride this out and not let it get to me."

"I can take all the time I need right now to let go and relax."

"I've survived other situations like this before, and I'll survive this one too."

"My anxiety/fear/sadness won't kill me; it just doesn't feel good right now."

"These are just my feelings, and eventually they'll go away."

"I'ts okay to feel sad/anxious/afraid sometimes."

"My thoughts don't control my life, I do."

"I can think differnt thoughts if I want to."

"I'm not in danger right now."

"So what?"

"This situation sucks, but it's only temporary."

"I'm strong and I can deal with this."

Relationship Satisfaction

	1 very dissatisfied	2 slightly dissatisfied	3 neutral	4 slightly satisfied	5 very satisfied
Communication & Openness					
Resolving Conflicts & Arguments					
Degree of Affection & Care					
Intimacy & Closeness					
Trust & Dependability					
Satisfaction with Your Role in the Relationships					
Satisfaction with the other Person's Role					
Overall Satisfaction with Your Relationship					
Total Scores					

Total Score	
7-11	Very Dissatisfied
12-18	Slightly Dissatisfied
19-25	Neutral
26-32	Slightly Satisfied
33-35	Very Satisfied

Medical Support

Remember when I decided to take Xanax to calm my anxiety? Naturally, I was given many opinions leaning against my medical intake. I was highly encouraged to pray, to take natural remedies, pursue yoga and just change my lifestyle (diet, morning routine, gratitude meditation). These opinions came from people who I hadn't talked with in months or years. I needed to remember that I have good discernment, and that only I truly know my body and mind. I repeat, we should never fully rely on one form of support, but create a collaborative support system. When I decided to take Xanax, I also decided to intentionally practice more gratitude meditations each morning. Being other's growing concern for me circled a probable addiction and codependency on Xanax, I found accountability in my family and friends and I updated them daily on how many Xanax pills I'd taken that day. I had an end date in mind, and a plan in place with my EMDR therapist, to stop taking Xanax after a month of use.

I have also tried using Zoloft. At the end of the day, I did not like Zoloft for myself. The anti-depressant harmed my ability to sleep well, and the lack of, or interrupted sleep, was not helpful when I needed to work the next day. With my lifestyle, I could not find a balance with allowing my body to adjust to Zoloft while trying to maintain financial health and getting the sleep I needed in order to have a good day. Still, I decided to try it.

There are many opinions out there. It is very important that we remember that our own opinion weighs the most. If you do not know what to believe in, or what to try, know what you don't believe in and what you will or will not be flexible to try. If you decide on natural remedies for your mental health, and it does not work for you, fear not trying another route knowing that the goal is to maintain a better, healthier you.

While medical support is very beneficial, we must not be too codependent on the prescription drug. While using your prescribed medical support, be sure to intentionally practice coping, and recognizing your emotional stability at the same time.

List of Emotions

abandoned
abused
accepting
accepted
adored
afflicted
afraid
aggressive
alarmed
alert
alienated
alone
amazed
amused
angry
anguished
animated
annoyed
anzious
apathetic
appalled
apologetic
appreciated
argumentative
aroused
arrogant
ashamed
assertive
assured
astonished
awkward
bashful

beautiful
betrayed
bewildered
bitter
blessed
blissful
boastful
bold
bored
bothered
brave
broken
bubbly
bummed
burdened
calm
capable
cautious
certain
chastened
cheerful
cherished
chill
chirpy
cocky
comfortable
comforted
complicated
concerned
confident
confused
contet

controlled
courageous
cowardly
creative
crushed
cursed
caring
dazed
defeated
defenseless
defensive
delected
delighted
demoralized
dependent
depressed
desolate
desparing
desperate
despicable
despised
despondent
destroyed
determined
devious
diminshed
dirty
disabled
disappointed
disillusioned
disgusted
dismayed

distracted
distressed
disturbed
dominated
doomed
doubtful
drained
dull
earer
ecstatic
elated
embarrassed
empowered
empty
encouraged
energetic
enlightened
enlivened
enraged
enthusiastic
envious
esteemed
exasperated
excited
exhausted
exploited
exposed
fatigued
fearful
feisty
festive
flirtatious

List of Emotions

flustered
foolish
forced
forgiven
forgotten
forlorn
forsaken
fortunate
fragile
frantic
free
frightened
frisky
frustrated
glad
gleeful
grateful
great
grieved
guarded
guilty
happy
hateful
healed
heartbroken
helpless
hesitant
hopeful
hopeless
horrified
hostile
humiliated

hungry
hurt
hysterical
ignored
important
impulsive
incapable
incompetent
indecisive
indifferent
indignant
inefficient
inferior
infatuated
injured
irrational
insensitive
inspired
insulted
interested
intolerant
irritated
jealous
joyful
jubilant
judged
kind
lazy
liberated
lifeless
listless
lively

livid
lonely
lost
lousy
loved
loving
lowly
lucky
mad
melanchaly
merry
miserable
misinformed
mistreated
misunder-
stood
mortified
motivated
mournful
naughty
negative
neglected
nervous
neutral
nonchalant
numb
obsessed
offended
optimistic
overwhelmed
overjoyed
panicked

paralyzed
passionate
passive
pathetic
peaceful
perplexed
pessimistic
plain
playful
pleased
possessive
powerless
preoccupied
prepared
pressured
proud
proactive
provoked
puzzled
reassured
rebellious
refreshed
regretful
rejected
rejected
rejuvenated
relaxed
relieved
reluctant
resentful
respected
relentless

List of Emotions

righteous
sad
satisfied
scared
scattered
secure
self-assured
sensitive
serious
shaky
shy
sick
skeptical
smart
sneaky
sorrowful
sorry
spirited
spiteful
strong
strong-willed
stupid
submissive
successful
sulky
superior
supported
surprised
suspicious
sympathetic
tearful
tenacious

tense
terrified
thankful
thoughtful
threatened
thrilled
timid
tired
tormented
tortured
ugly
uncertain
uncomfortable
understood
uneasy
unhappy
uninterested
unpleasant
unprotected
unsafe
unsettled
unsure
upbeat
upset
useless
vaulnerable
vibrant
victimized
vivacious
vulnerable
weak
weary

woeful
wonderful
worried
worthless
worthy
wronged

My Negative Emotions

Emotion: "I feel UNLOVED"								
Abandonded	Desperate	Embarrassed	Forsaken		Hurt	Lifeless	Neglected	Sad
Crushed	Despised	Empty	Grieved		Ignored	Lonely	Numb	Ugly
Depressed	Diminshed	Forgotten	Heartbroken		Inferior	Lost	Rejected	Unhappy

BELIEF/THOUGHT			
"I can't"	"I'm not needed any-more"	"I'm not good enough for you"	"I might as well die"
"I don't count"	"Nobody wants me"	"You don't love me"	"I'm unlovable"
"I don't matter"	"What's wrong with me"	"Nobody cares"	"I'll never love again"
"I'm worthless"	"I'll just leave"	"You don't want me"	Other:

Emotion: "I feel INSUFFICIENT"						
Awkward	Defeated	Failure	Helpless	Inadequate	Inferior	Powerless
Bored	Dejected	Frustrated	Hopeless	Indecisive	Pathetic	Unmotivated

BELIEF/THOUGHT	
"I'ts too hard"	"No matter what I do..."
"What's the use"	"I'll never get it right"
"What if I fail"	"I can't do anything about it"
"I can't do it right"	"I'm stupid"
"I can't do it by myself"	Other:

My Negative Emotions

Emotion: "I feel ANGRY"							
Aggressive	Appalled	Bitter	Disgusted	Hostile	Insulted	Jealous	Offended
Angry	Argumentative	Defensive	Entraged	Hysterical	Intolerant	Judged	Pessimistic
Annoyed	Arrogant	Devious	Hateful	Impulsive	Irritated	Mistreaed	Provoked
BELIEF/THOUGHT							

"I hate this"	"How could you do that"	"Not again"	"Everyone's out to get me"
"You did it on purpose"	"I'll never forgive you"	"I deserve better"	"I'm about to lose it"
"That isn't fair"	"You should be ashamed"	"Why did this happen to me"	"I can't control myself"
"I'm a victim"	"You are terrible"	"I have the worst luck"	Other:

Emotion: "I feel GUILTY"					
Ashamed	Regret	Sorrow	Self-Hatred	Sinful	Regretful
Embarrassed	Shame	Humiliated	Remorseful	Blameworthy	Contrite
BELIEF/THOUGHT					

"I'ts too hard"	"No matter what I do..."
"What's the use"	"I'll never get it right"
"What if I fail"	"I can't do anything about it"
"I can't do it right"	"I'm stupid"
"I can't do it by myself"	Other:

Describe Your Emotion

Name your emotion.

_____

Describe your emotion, or draw a picture on one of the blank pages in the back of this book.

_____

_____

_____

Describe the intensity of your emotion.

_____

_____

Describe the quality of your emotion.

_____

_____

Describe your thoughts related to your emotion.

_____

_____

_____

_____

Recognize Your Emotion

What Happened? Describe the situation:

_____

_____

_____

When did this happen and where were you?

_____

_____

Why do you think the situation happened?

_____

_____

How did that situation make you feel, both emotionally & physically?

_____

_____

_____

What did you want to do as a result of that feeling?

_____

_____

_____

Goals

My goal is:

_____

_____

_____

_____

My target date is:

_____

To reach my goal, I will take these steps:

_____

_____

_____

_____

_____

When I feel like giving up, I will:

_____

_____

_____

_____

_____

CREDITS

@debijean.silentsong

DEBI MCMURRAY
Editor

@esthervivankay

ESTHER KAY
Editor

@mollyjanephotography

MOLLY JANE
Photographer

@maias_north

MATT GROTHE
Photographer

@danikanoelcreative

DANIKA NOEL
Book Designer, Marketing & Branding

@nicolette_v_metz

NICOLETTE VAUGHN
Cover Design

A special thank you to the following, for your valuable support and unconditional love over the years. When I imagine you and all you have done to make me feel safe, important and worthy, I know I wouldn't have made it without your help. I appreciate you and your work more than you know. Thank you!

Prisoner's of Hope Healing Ministry of
The International House of Prayer, Kansas City

Wildflower Ministries
with Carol Grina and Vicki Pollard

Avila University, Staff & Classmates

Maria & The Kangas Family
Penny & The Regier Family
Sarah & The Hacker Family
Ariel & The Pankonin Family
Lyn & The Clark Family
Cecelia & The Erholtz & Hoskins Family
Jacqui Floding & Family
The Dahlgren Family
Kristen & The Moon Family
Carron & The Montgomery Family

Meresa Schroeder, Adria Oak, Stacey Seeger, Tabiatha Branden, Beka Enoch, Ana Vogt, Grandma Jan, Aunty Doreen, Grandma Sharron and Grandpa Dennis, Aunty Vonnie, Aunty Jeannie, Mary Olson, Kelly Phillips, Danika Noel, Debi McMurray, Esther Kay, Sarah Pender, Ta Fett, Phil Bohlander, "Cari Madison", Zack Hensley, Teresa McClain, Mary Pope, Mike & Anne Rizzo, and so many more.

Thank you!